Carl
All Re Uses

iT iS WHAT iT iS

A TRUE MANHATTAN REAL ESTATE NiGHTMARE WITH A SiLVER LiNiNG

BY COLIN RATH

Copyright @ 2015 Colin Rath
ALL RIGHTS RESERVED

All photos and illustrations copyright Colin Rath

No part of this book may be reproduced in any manner without the express
written consent of the author except in the case of brief excerpts in critical
reviews and articles. All inquiries should be addressed to the contact
information listed on this website:
www.colinrath.com

ISBN-10: 978-0-692-39772-5
ISBN-13: 0-692397728

Cover Designer: Krasimir Galabov, www.targetmktng.com
Book Designer: Miguel Trindade, www.targetmktng.com
Development Editor: Alexander Lindroth, www.targetmktng.com

**I would like to dedicate
this book to the people who
believed in us:**

Mr. George (Tim) Rath & Mrs. Barbara J Rath

Mr. Samuel Harvey & Mrs. Eleanor Harvey

Mr. Patrick Daly

Mr. Andy Albstein,
who saved my home & family

**Some debts you never
can fully repay**

Colin Rath is awake.

Colin Rath is always awake. He never rests anymore. Not really. When his head hits the pillow, his mind rushes to his desk, figuring, calculating, turning numbers inside out to see if there is something he missed the last eighty times he checked. Adding and subtracting, evaluating and discarding, desperately striving to come up with the solution he knows is out there... somewhere.

There must be a way out of this thing. There must be.

Colin Rath is in hell, right here on Earth. Doomed to suffer interminably for committing that most unforgivable of modern American sins.

The sin of believing.

Believing that a person's word is his bond. Believing in bankers and contracts and contractors. Believing that blood is thicker than water. Believing that if you do things the right way, it'll all work out in the end.

Colin is paying for his sin, with interest compounded daily. But it's not all bad.

Because he knows that to Persevere will save him in the end.

DOUG ELLIOTT

TABLE OF CONTENTS

IT IS
WHAT IT IS

PREFACE

My generation, as a whole, never suffered any real financial hardship until 2007. No Great Depressions, no World Wars. We grew up with all the perks and toys that came along with being natural-born citizens of the world's leading consumer nation during the longest economic expansion period in history. Sure, there were wars and crises, but George W. Bush advised us to buy stuff as our way to help the war effort. Tough job but someone had to do it. So we sucked it up and went out and bought BMWs and Sub-Zero fridges. Take that, Bin Laden.

On a personal level, I can say that my life was pretty damn good prior to '07. In 1996, I married Pam, the love of my life, and launched into a six-year renovation of one of the last brownstones to sell for under a million dollars in Chelsea, Manhattan. We were both working full time, traveled extensively and had begun a family. "To paraphrase the popular song, the future, so bright you had to wear shades".

Manhattan real estate started to boom and eventually became the construction bellwether for the entire nation, showing annual double-digit appreciation for the next decade. When Pam and I finished the full restoration of our brownstone, it was right in the middle of the construction boom. Our building had appreciated over 700 percent. So we got caught up in the fever like everyone else and bought the building next door. The banks were throwing money around like comedy club coupons in Times Square; it seemed downright un-American not to accept some of it. Pam and I decided to combine our recently finished building with the adjacent building, which was in major disrepair, to develop the first green, cantilevered condominium complex in Manhattan.

"Green design" was the new obsession of the architectural world and our project was all that and a tank of biofuel. Our development at 121-123 West 15th Street incorporated two geothermal wells, passive solar radiant heating, reclaimed natural materials, modular construction, a car lift to a private garage, and Nana doors in its ultra-modern design. It was the Green Dream on steroids. But the Rath Family Dream was even cooler, if I do say so myself. Our long-range plan was to develop this building for my expanding family, live there for a few years, and make some money selling the other condo units. Then, when the kids were old enough, sell our own unit, climb aboard our boat, and sail around the world together for a few years on a journey of exploration to look for a new locality to call home for our family.

Both dreams went up in flames one fateful day in November, 2006, two years into construction, when an event occurred that unearthed a major multi-contractor fraud on our site. That revelation put the project twelve months behind and $3.5 Million over budget on the eve of the housing balloon burst. It would eventually sink us thirteen million dollars in debt, destroy my credit rating for the rest of my natural life, tie me up in lawsuits, and force our home into foreclosure.

This is the story of our determination. How my family was battered, bruised, beaten, and left by the side of the road to die. Yet, how we managed to crawl to safety. Wiser, ornerier, and far less innocent. Turns out, the flames of failure didn't destroy our vision. They only toughened it. Like tempered steel.

As we struggled to salvage our project, Pam and I went through many of the same ordeals millions of homeowners have recently gone through, except that ours were magnified a hundredfold. Why? Because of the staggering dollar figures involved and because this was Manhattan, which meant dealing not only with the typical array of banks, lawyers, and insurance companies, but also with entrenched rent-controlled tenants, politicians, the Department of Buildings, the Department of Transportation, OSHA, the New York Times, the Department of Housing, local "watchdog" types with too much time on their hands, high-stakes bankers, criminals, sophisticated conmen, arbitrators, and an array of highly specialized contractors, suppliers, architects, manufacturers, fixers and expeditors that would make your head spin.

Pam and I were not professional real estate developers. This was our home. We both worked full time and lived on the construction site the entire time, while raising three young girls. When everything went south, it affected us in a very personal way. We hope this story of our family's perseverance through a decade of unbelievable challenges will serve as an inspiration to you any time you're feeling overwhelmed, disillusioned, or beaten down.

If we could get through this, with our dignity and sanity intact, then anyone can get through anything. Seriously.

THIS IS WHAT IT IS.

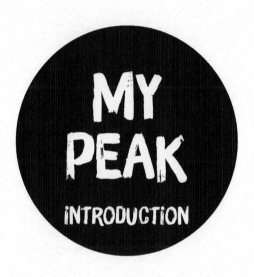

MY
PEAK

INTRODUCTION

> **"** *He who risks and fails can be forgiven. He who never risks and never fails is a failure in his whole being.*
>
> *Paul Tillich*

My friends and I often say that some of our buddies peaked early. You know the types: quarterback of the high school football team, got the hottest girl, and now has a pillow-sized beer gut and hasn't worked for years. Or the young hotshot who made his early mark in the business world, raking in the money, Porsche in the circular driveway, and now idles away in a boring career. You've seen the story before. How did I get here?

I remember the exact moment my life peaked. I keep a picture of it on my screen saver to remind me daily of a lesson learned.

My personal Kilimanjaro—the one I've been scrambling to re-attain and surpass ever since—happened on Labor Day weekend, 2006. The start of the Stamford Yacht Club Vineyard Race, the foremost sailboat race on Long Island Sound. Why the start of the race and not the finish? Well, therein lies the yarn.

The Vineyard is a sailboat race from Stamford, CT, around the Martha's Vineyard lighthouse, and back to Stamford. Some 197 miles by water. My sailboat Googolplex (X-412) was having its best racing season ever, after three years of hard teamwork, and was poised to take the NORT (Northern Ocean Racing Trophy). It would be the first time a production boat, not a one-design yacht, would win the trophy since the race's inception in 1961. We were in first place for the trophy; no one could beat us going into the race. All Googolplex had to do was finish the Vineyard regatta and we won NORT.

Racing-wise, I had the hottest boat on Long Island Sound.

Personally and professionally, I was sailing even hotter. I had a wife that was beautiful and three healthy daughters, I was running a successful direct mail and fulfillment business, and was hip deep in my building project at 121-123 West 15th Street in Manhattan. I'd managed to get my hands on $13 million in development funds and was forging ahead with my wildly ambitious Green Dream building. Somehow I had borrowed my way into becoming a bona fide Manhattan real estate developer who was writing a new definition in green construction. How awesome was that?

But today was not a day for business. Today was a race day.

It was the last qualifying regatta for the trophy. We had sailed Googolplex well that year and collected lots of silver. In 2006 she took first overall in the Block Island Race, fourth IRC and PHRF in the Newport-Bermuda Race (sixteenth out of 168 overall), Fourth in Class in the 100th Anniversary Bermuda Regatta, first overall in the Stamford Stratford Shoal race, and seventh overall in Onion Patch. All Googolplex had to do, today, was finish the Vineyard race and we won the NORT. We didn't have to win or beat any specific boats, just finish the damn race.

Maybe that was the problem. Failure seemed impossible. But it turns out nothing is guaranteed. Weather is nature's way of reminding us of that. In racing and in other things.

The race weather forecast was for gale force winds, over 50 knots, with wave crests breaking seven feet. Conditions were going to get progressively worse as the race went on, with no relief in sight.

There were fifty boats on the starting line.

Twelve hours later only four remained. The good news was, Googolplex was amongst them.

In the dark of the night, we limped into Port Jefferson Harbor without a proper storm jib and with a host of nautical ailments. We needed to reorganize, get out of the storm for a while, and whip the boat back into racing form. Under sail we dropped anchor. Half the crew was seasick and had already painted the hull with pizza from lunch. We decided to wait till daybreak to jump back into the race. I tried to stay focused on what needed to be done, constantly checking the web tracking online and formulating various time-lapse scenarios to finish the race, but motivation and morale was ebbing among the crew. Meanwhile the storm was increasing in intensity.

Mentally, I began to slip out of race mode and to allow real-world problems back into my consciousness. The worst thing you can do in a regatta. The thing about sailboat racing—and the reason I love it—is you leave all your problems onshore and focus purely on making your boat the fastest vessel out there. Period. Nothing else. You and your crew constantly trim and make tactical decisions with that one simple goal in mind. Thirteen people working together as a unit, calling wind shifts, changing sails, watching the competition, checking the weather and tides. No distractions allowed.

By daybreak, we had made a storm jib out of a staysail and everyone had gotten enough sleep to get back in the race. We sailed past the breakwater off Port Jefferson and were beating upwind to Plum Gut when the wind actually increased in force to over 55 knots and the waves became eight-foot rollers. So we kept at it for another hour, edging down the sound, but we were not making any headway. The problem was, the race had a finite completion time of Sunday at midnight. Our challenge became one of not having enough time to complete the course. And once we made it to Block Island Sound, the storm effects would worsen because we'd be more open to the ocean. Plus my crew was getting seasick again and just wasn't up for it anymore.

So we turned around and radioed the race committee of our withdrawal and headed into Port Jefferson for a hot lunch. That was the last time I sailed Googolplex.

I still believe that if we had put up the storm trysail and pushed through, we would have made it. Because once we made it to the turning mark, the wind would have been behind us as a reach tack and we would have flown back to Stamford. Which is exactly what we did after lunch—we made it from Port Jefferson to Stamford in record time, going 15-16 knots.

But, as they say, would have, should have, and could have are the best brokers in the business.

I sold the boat three months later to buy an elevator for my building project at 123 West 15th Street. I furled my sails... in more ways than one.

"*The greatest loss is when you are no longer hungry and no longer foolish.*

Susan Sarandon
(my former neighbor on 15th Street)

The last night I slept was November 16, 2006, I mean really slept, out cold through the night in a deep REM cycle. The kind of sleep where you wake up refreshed and invigorated and raring to go. Especially since today was Friday.

The call that came at 7:15 a.m. on November 17, 2006 changed all that forever.

Early that morning, I awoke around 5:30, as I always do, to go to work. Soon as my ears awoke you heard thunder and the constant cascade of water. It was pouring rain, my mood went dark quickly from the get-go. The roads would be already be flooded. Your typical November New York/New England day. Not quite freezing, constant heavy rain, and generally miserable to be outside. The radio said the West Side Highway was flooded. That meant the Henry Hudson Parkway would be out of commission too. So I would have to take the FDR to 95, up to Stamford, CT. Which is always entertaining in a heavy rain because all the SUV's think that their 4 x 4's have the same traction going 70 in any weather and usually end up running into each other causing more traffic jams. At the time I had been doing the reverse commute for more than sixteen years. Manhattan to Stamford. This drive became old, 10 years ago, but I am not ready for the slow death of living in the burbs. So I do the commute to keep the excitement of living in the city of five million.

My family of five was living in our condo at 121 West 15th Street (between 6th & 7th Ave) in Manhattan—the brownstone we had renovated from top to bottom—and Pam, my wife (no, she hates that word; "my better half" as she likes to say), and I were deeply into the reclamation project of the building next door, at 123 West 15th. You'll be hearing a lot more about 123 West 15th Street as this story unfolds, but all you really need to know for now is that the foundation contractor, Plumb Level & Square LLC, had a cement pour scheduled for the front foundation that day. I had already learned that, due to the rain, it would have to be scrubbed. This only added major disappointment to an already dismal start of to the day. This was more bad news because Plumb Level & Square was already far behind schedule and the owner Richie needed to do this pour today to get back in the game. We needed another setback like a sailboat needs a hurricane. The project was two years into construction at this point and struggling mightily to stay on track. This was his last chance.

The foundation was to be based on twelve pilings that were built of steel rebar and cement at depths of 8 to 12 feet below the basement floor grade. Each of these pilings was designed to rest on solid bedrock to support the building's steel structure. This was extremely important because the building was going up eight stories and then cantilevering over 20 feet to the east. Without the pilings tied into the bedrock, the building would eventually fall over. It might happen slowly over several years, but it would happen. The pilings-on-bedrock concept was the key to the whole structure. The twelve pilings had already been constructed; the next step was to tie them into the foundation slab, making it one solid structure.

As I said, the contractors were way behind. In fact, they were on the verge of being dismissed. I already had another team on tap to take over the work and get us back on schedule if PL & S didn't turn around soon. Our contact with PL & S stipulated that the foundation was to be done by September 21, 2006. It was mid-November now and winter was coming on fast. We needed to get the foundation finished pronto or it was going to set us back till spring. This is where a Performance Bond would have paid off. A performance bond is an insurance policy that if the work is not completed as contracted the bond pays for any cost caused by the delay, thereby in theory making you whole, no losses. But it is expensive, in our case it would have been $85,000 had we taken one out. Any delay was not an option when you're carrying thirteen million in loans at a dizzying daily interest rate. I was going to make the decision to change foundation contractors this weekend. The weather made up my mind for me.

"Pressure pushing down on me - Pressing down on you no man ask for -Under pressure that brings a building down -Splits a family in two -Puts people on streets" - resounded in my mind as sung by Mr. David Bowie .

That morning, Ace an employee of Plumb Level & Square was working on the front foundation setting up the wood frame for the cement pour. Ace was one of the three day workers that had been working on my buildings for over a decade by then. A reliable cat from the East Village, He had got there early because he knew PL & S needed to get this pour done to keep the job. His hard work didn't deserve the tough break he got that day, literally.

The original schist foundation from 1853 still remained intact and the contractors had excavated underneath it completely. This old foundation wall wasn't made of solid schist (which I'll explain in a minute), but rather, chunks of 150 year old schist stacked and mortared together, much like the stone walls you see all around New York and New England. The old wall was now completely exposed underneath and propped up with a few beams here and there for support and "safety." The contractors had dug out five feet directly below this schist wall to frame out a grade beam—that's a reinforced concrete beam that distributes the load from the bearing wall onto the piling caps. The grade beam was to extend the length of the lot, 20 feet from east to west, enclosed with steel rebar that tied into the vertical pilings. It was all to be secured together like a table, with the "legs" being the pilings attached to the bedrock, eight to ten feet below ground level.

Ace got to the site early that morning, around 5:00 a.m., and was doing some final digging out for the front form under the original schist foundation. This was all during the deluge. Water, of course, has a way of making things shift. Witness, for example, the Grand Canyon.

The call that changed my life came in at 7:15, shortly after I arrived at the office of Better Lists, Inc, the family-founded company I ran in Stamford.

"Pam, what's up?" I said, grabbing my cell phone.

"It's not good, Colin," replied Pam. "Ace got hurt. Pretty bad."

"The guy on Richie's crew?"

"Right. That old schist wall let go and he was under it. He's lucky to be alive."

"What? How did that happen? I thought they had that thing secured. How is he?" I asked, a sick feeling of dread tugging at my chest.

"It looks like just his leg," Pam said, "but it's bad. Definitely broken, maybe worse."

"Do we need to take him to…"

"No, he's already on his way to the hospital. Richie showed up at the door a minute ago, told me what had happened. Asked me to call an ambulance." Remember, we lived in the property adjacent to the construction site, so our home was like base headquarters to the crew. "They just got here. St. Vincent's is only two blocks away. He should be there in no time."

"I'm on my way."

"There's nothing you can do here," Pam pointed out, and I realized she was right. Ace was being taken care of. Other than that, things were now out of our hands. Sickeningly so, in fact. You see, when you call an ambulance to a construction site, the fire department shows up and OSHA (Occupational Safety and Health Administration) is immediately notified. Once OSHA arrives, the first thing they do is close the site for investigation.

So that was that. We were screwed. Nothing more could be done today—or anytime soon—from the site. Everything would be shut down, frozen in place until there was at least a preliminary finding from the OSHA team.

As best as I can determine, here's what happened that morning:

After an hour or so of digging under the schist wall, Ace heard a rumble and that was when "the schist hit the fan." The entire 5-foot-high, 20-foot-long, 2-foot-deep rock wall above him gave way. Most likely the rainwater had loosened something, or maybe it was just a cumulative result of too much digging out underneath without enough shoring up, but something shifted and all hell broke loose. Rocks started dropping out of the wall, from the bottom up. Lucky for Ace, he was alert and agile. He scrambled out of the way of largest rocks and only his leg got caught in the falling wall. It could have been much, much worse. This was a wall of 50- to 100-pound rocks raining down a distance of 5 to 8 feet. His leg got fractured in two places, clean break.

The good news was that in six to eight weeks he was going to be fine.

The same, alas, could not be said for our project. Or for my peace of mind. I knew the accident was going to be a major setback, but I had no idea at the time that this simple rockslide would snowball into an avalanche that would derail my life, family, business, friendships, and everything I had ever believed in, as well as deal a death blow to Terrapin Industries, the development company I'd started. I had no inkling that the moment that wall collapsed, my mental and emotional peace would disintegrate along with it. This was the start of our "new normal" for the next seven years (but who's counting?). Sleep would soon become a matter of brief, stolen snatches of shallow delta brainwaves when my mind and body were too exhausted to function any longer. (On the plus side, I've learned that three o'clock in the morning is one of the best times to communicate by email with your attorney. They're usually up reading briefs or fretting over something and you get their full attention. But I digress...)

As expected, the construction site remained shut down. For the moment all we could do was wait for the site inspectors to file their report with OSHA and the Department of Buildings to file theirs. Once that had happened, we'd be able to get copies of the reports. Then we would know how deep a hole we had to climb out of and how far behind our schedule was going to be. I couldn't imagine how we were going to get this all resolved in time to get the foundation poured before winter set in.

At the time I thought that was our biggest problem. I dream about those days now.

The first thing I did was call my expeditor, Andy Pisani, at Metropolis Group. An expeditor, in case you've never worked with one, is just what its name implies. It's a person who helps you navigate the endless maze of paperwork, permits, and approvals involved in trying to build a building, especially in Manhattan. An expeditor knows the system, knows the people, and knows the strategies and tactics that work. He's an expert on resolving coding and zoning violations. Andy also had been working with me since I redid 121 West 15th street in 1998. He is a little younger than me, slim Italian man with brown hair. All that running around the DOB kept him in shape. I would be one of several clients that he was working for simultaneously so he was constantly on the move. Always very professional and helpful. He knew we were in trouble now and jumped in right away to help us dig out of this hole,

Anyway, I got in touch with Andy and told him to start the process of getting our violations cleared up. The first step was to get an appointment with the DOB (Department of Buildings). It takes at least three weeks for the DOB to get back to you with a meeting date. Then, when they do get back to you, the meetings usually set for another two to three weeks down the road. So you're talking six or seven weeks just to sit down with these people. That's why the earlier you request a meeting the better. Even if you don't know what your violations are yet, you immediately get to work setting up the meeting. For me, speed was critical. I had thirteen million dollars in loans at a 13% interest rate (Yes, Hard Money folks), which meant I'd be losing five grand a day while the construction site sat idle. I couldn't afford to waste a minute ($3.26 per minute, to be precise—in case you were wondering).

After Andy got things rolling, we nervously awaited the report from DOB. Once we finally got the report in hand, the real horror story began to unfold...

CHAPTER TWO

FRAUD UNEARTHED

> *It is possible to commit no errors and still lose. That is not a weakness. That is life.*
>
> Captain Picard
> of the USS Enterprise

As soon as I could get everyone together, I accompanied my architect Alexander Gendell (Sasha) my foundation engineers, and my new contractor, Superior Contracting & Masonry, to the site to look at the remediation list from the DOB and figure out what we needed to do to get this back on schedule. Also with us was Howard Trueger, the owner's rep I'd hired to oversee the construction project. Why had I hired Howard? Well, even though Pam and I lived at the site, we still had to go to work every day and we needed someone who knew what they were doing to watch over the construction process with a professional eye. Plus, he was an old sailing buddy that really needed a job, so I helped him out in hopes that it would work out for the both of us. That is where Howard came in. Dressed in business shirts and khakis, He commuted daily from Hoboken to the job site. He was a disbarred attorney who loved to tell stories with his deep smoker's voice while adjusting his wire brimmed glasses. Unfortunately Howard could while the day away with small talk, but more on that later. Theoretically. he was supposed to be my daily eyes and ears on the site to confirm that all the contractors' work was done correctly.

The reason the project was closed down, the report from DOB informed us, was for failure to properly protect the site during excavation. That was why the wall supposedly fell on Ace. Tough to argue the point when you looked at the site up close and personal. The bottom of the schist wall—what was left of it—sat there basically suspended in space, with nothing except a few strategically placed beams to prevent it from collapsing. Imagine digging out a septic tank hole under an old fieldstone wall in your yard and relying on a few wedged logs to hold the wall in place. That was essentially what Plumb Level & Square had done on our site.

"Howard," I said, shaking my head in disbelief, "you should have been all over these guys about this. That's why I hired you. How could you not notice a wall suspended in empty space like this? How could you not know this would lead to problems?"

To his credit, Howard didn't try to defend himself. He just put his hands in his worn khakis pockets and studied his work boots as if they held the secret to cold fusion. Clearly he had failed to do his job. But it was of no use to point fingers now. Besides, it was ultimately the contractors' responsibility to protect the site. They hadn't come close to doing so, it seemed. And really, in the end it was my responsibility for putting my trust in this particular contractor. Now was the time to figure out a quick resolution to this mess and finish the building ASAP.

It was revealed much later that remnants of an underground stream, or more likely a stream that had been built over, existed on the edge of 123 West 15th Street. That was what had caused the initial problem, but failure to resolve it was what had magnified it to epic portions. When Plumb Level & Square began digging out the foundation, the forms would slowly fill with water. Of course, pouring cement into a water pit isn't good. The solution would have been to pump out the forms and keep the pump going until the cement was dry. That was all that needed to be done. Simple. Had it been brought to light by Howard, or by PL &S, or by CTL when it was found, this would have never been an issue. Unfortunately, you can't trust anything or anyone anymore—in the construction trades or in any other business these days.

It turned out that shoring up the old foundation was the least of the things Plumb Level & Square had screwed up. A much bigger issue would soon reveal itself.

Before I get into that, let me say a few words about bedrock. And I don't mean Fred Flintstone's hometown. I mean the substance that lies at the heart of all construction in Manhattan. It's an important thing to understand.

In case you didn't know, Manhattan is basically a giant rock. That is why it has one of the most amazing skylines in the world. Because of its bedrock foundation, it is a natural site for vertical construction. Tall buildings. The more solid the base, naturally, the taller you can build. Manhattan's skyscrapers are all a direct result of having this incredibly strong, solid rock base that makes New York pretty unique in the world.

New York's bedrock consists of several different types of stone. There's Fordham Gneiss, which can be found under the Bronx, Inwood Marble, and most famous of all, Manhattan Schist. Schist is a particularly strong and durable rock, well-suited for anchoring tall buildings. It formed about 450 million years ago when a massive continental collision drove a layer of shale about nine miles deep into the Earth. Long story short, intense heat and pressure transformed the shale into a tough metamorphic rock—full of mica, quartz, feldspar, and hornblende—known as schist. Eons later, the tectonic plates shifted again, pushing the newly minted schist back up to the surface. Manhattan was the proud recipient of a major slab of this stuff.

What makes schist desirable from a construction standpoint—if I understand my geology correctly—is that its mineral components, most notably the mica, are aligned in fairly long pieces. This gives the material good tensile strength but also makes it easy to break up into sheet-like chunks, much like the shale it formed from. So not only can you anchor buildings with it, but you can use it as a construction material to build walls and foundations. Like the one that fell on Ace's leg.

As for anchoring buildings in New York:

Short, relatively lightweight buildings only a few stories high don't generally need to be anchored in bedrock. For taller buildings, going up to around twenty stories or so, you can lay pilings on top of the schist layer. For really tall buildings, you need to drill down into the schist and anchor the building right in the bedrock. In our case, our building was small enough that we probably wouldn't have needed to go to bedrock if it had been a traditional design. But because we had chosen to go the cantilevered route, that changed the requirement. We needed to tie our pilings directly to the bedrock.

As we were looking around the foundation site that morning, Alexander (Sasha), the architect, stopped in his tracks and pointed in the direction of one of the pilings. The rainstorm had washed away a lot of the dirt in the foundation pit and had exposed a foundation piling in its entirety. His jaw dropped like a tractor bucket and the expression that came over his face made my heart skip a beat. One glance at the piling told the whole story. It was a story both impossible to ignore and impossible to process. Even though Alexander had only a few projects under his belt, he knew this was a major problem. Sasha was young kid back then. He didn't have his license yet. He was working under his father's who signed off on all the filed drawings. Sasha was a young brash architect just starting out making a name for himself, married with kid on the way. He always dressed well European continental style with some designer glasses that worked with his brown hair color. He had talent and eventually designed a line of folding furniture called Folditure". You can find more on him at http://www.gendella.com/

"Am I seeing what I think I'm seeing?" someone blurted out.

"I hope not," said the guy from Superior Contracting, "'cause I'm thinkin' this has got to be a hallucination."

After a moment's pause, someone else said, "I need a drink." I think it might have been me.

The piling we were looking at was not even close to bedrock! Not even close. Bedrock in this part of the city lay only twelve feet below ground level, and it was obvious to the naked eye that the piling stopped six feet short of it. There was no way this could be a simple oversight on the part of Plumb Level & Square. You don't just accidentally fail to complete the single most essential aspect of the job. Building to bedrock was the entire purpose for sinking the pilings. Without that, the building would collapse.

Yet here was one of our pilings suspended in dirt, high above the rock it was supposed to be resting on. This was intentional fraud.

How could this be? There'd been too many checks and balances in place for this kind of "error" to happen. After all, we hadn't just taken PL&S at their word. We had hired an independent third-party inspector, Certified Testing Labs, to verify their work. And CTL's signed certificates were sitting in my office. CTL's certificates approved the construction process along the schedule of work completed. So we had no reason to even suspect such a failure was possible. I remembered the day the inspector from Certified Testing Labs had shown up to do his work. It was quite a thing to behold: in order to make his certification that the pilings were built to bedrock, he'd had to physically crawl inside the form for each piling beam with a rock hammer and actually chip off a piece of bedrock, then sign a statement attesting to the fact that the piling was indeed built to bedrock. He had to show physical proof.

We had his bedrock chips. We had his certifications. The only thing we didn't have was a piling that rested on bedrock. None of this made sense.

Of course, once you question one piling, you have to question them all. As I began to realize the kind of trouble we were looking at, I could feel panic creeping across my skin like cold slime mold. Seven feet of concrete had already been poured over the bases of most of the pilings! If we were going to be forced to re-examine, and possible redo, all the pilings, this would represent an unthinkable setback in terms of both time and money. There was no budget for that kind of remediation. No time, either. Not at $5000 a day in interest.

I couldn't wrap my mind around a problem of this magnitude.

A smart man would have stopped right here, thrown in the towel, and redesigned the building to work with this modified foundation. Finished it as quickly as possible and gotten the hell out of there. Sold the whole thing and chalked it up as a learning experience. The foundation probably would have

been fine for a standard building construction. But I was fixated on building my cantilevered dream home. Bad as things looked, I wasn't ready to give up that dream.

I pulled myself out of panic mode and reviewed my options. After talking to a couple of my resident experts, I somehow convinced myself it wouldn't take that long to correct the problem and get back on schedule. So I decided to ignore the acid burning a hole in my gut and put a claim in on my insurance. I was going to seek compensation for this mess, damn it, and keep moving full-steam ahead.

When was the last time you ignored your gut and had a happy result?

My first phone call was to The Hartford, the company that carried my builder's risk insurance on the construction. My second call was to Plumb Level & Square's insurance company (Phoenix). I notified them both that I was initiating claims against them. Both insurance companies were courteous and told me they'd be sending out an agent to look at the site. Both assured me I would get a quick response as to the extent of their coverage. Both were shoveling pure Manhattan bullshit, as it turned out. I think BS401 is a core course requirement for the job.

The next phone call was to Certified Testing Labs, where I spoke to Richard Zaloum, the owner and manager. Needless to say, I was a bit "animated" on the phone with him. In the back of my mind, I was still hoping for a miracle of some kind; hoping that somehow only one piling had been mis-certified and he could offer me assurances of that. He suggested that we meet in person. This would be the first time I actually met him, I only talked to him on the phone and emailed corresponded with him extensively over the year.

A gray haired overweight Sicilian looking man with a friendly face in a CTL polo company shirt arrived at my office on the site. Richard had one of those shit kicking smiles that you know he used to get away with everything. The kind of smiles that he could use to tell you it's raining while he pisses on your leg. He was a good old boy who had been in the business since the pyramids were built and surveyed. He definitely knew all the tricks. Armed with photographs of the faulty piling and statements from a couple of my experts, I gave him a full tour of the foundation. Once Zaloum realized there was no point defending his company's actions, the conversation went something like this (as best I can recall it):

"It's an unfortunate situation," Zaloum owned, "but what you have to understand is that our inspectors are not legally bound by their verifications."

"Excuse me?" I said. I had been prepared for this guy to do some pretty creative verbal tap-dancing, but I hadn't seen that one coming. "What do you mean, 'not bound'?"

"Let me explain exactly what you purchase when you contract for our services," he said with a note of weary impatience in his voice, as if he were trying to teach String Theory to a night-shift worker at Burger King. "When we send someone out to your site to do an inspection, all we're really offering you is a second opinion, based on the best of that inspector's knowledge."

"Oh? Then would you mind telling me what the word 'certified' means?" I inquired politely.

"Essentially, the inspector certifies that what he has written on the paper is indeed his opinion," said Zaloum. "He can't certify that reality actually corresponds to his opinion."

"What are you talking about?" I asked, my Irish blood starting to simmer. "What are all these little rock chips and signed certificates all about? What the hell did I pay you for?"

"What my company provides, as its core service, is the peace of mind of knowing your construction job was done properly."

"But it wasn't!" I pointed out.

"In your case, regrettably not. Again, that is unfortunate."

"So what do you plan to do about it?"

"Unfortunately..." Zaloum said, stretching out his favorite word like it was Coney Island taffy, "the company itself cannot be held responsible for anything our inspectors certify. All with a smile of a Cheshire cat. Our role is essentially that of brokers, not employers. All we really do is facilitate a connection between you and a qualified inspector. What the inspector does on site is out of our hands. But in the interest of good customer relations, I'm prepared to offer you this for your troubles."

Like a mobster slipping a politician a bribe, he slid an envelope across my desk. It contained a check for $25,000. I slid it back to him.

Twenty-five thousand! Five day's interest on my $13,000,000 loans. I was not amused. Besides, did he really think I'd take a check from him after he'd already given me phony rock chips and phony certificates? (In hindsight I should have kept the money and considered it a deposit on the suit against him.)

Later, in the discovery phase of my lawsuit against him, I would learn that his company had done the exact same thing to another developer five years earlier when certifying the work on an automobile garage in midtown Manhattan. That building did fall down—because, surprise, surprise, the foundation pilings were not in bedrock—and Zaloum was sued and lost in a settlement of $5,000,000. Of course, it was his insurance company that ended up paying, not Zaloum. What did Zaloum do? He pulled up stakes and started a new company under a different name. Don't ask me how he ever got another insurance policy after that. But I guess that was his business model. Collect your fees, hand out phony certifications until you get caught, then cry no mas, stick your insurance company with the bill, and change the name of your company. Rinse and repeat.

Certified Testing Labs was an outright fraud. But one with a real office, a real website, credible employees, testimonials, and a Yellow Pages presence. Operating in the broad light of day.

Welcome to the construction industry in New York.

All hope for a speedy resolution went flitting out the window after the Zaloum visit. Not only had my foundation guys been frauds, but the company certifying them had a hidden history of fraudulent work. I wondered if money had changed hands between Certified Testing Labs and Plumb Level & Square, and how much.

What kills me as I look back is that I took great pains to do everything right. I didn't try to cut corners or cheap out. First, I hired a foundation company that I had every reason to believe were experts in their field and had worked with me on the foundation of my first building three years prior. Then I hired an owner's rep/project manager, Howard Trueger, to keep an eye on them. On top of that, I hired an independent testing company, Certified Testing Labs, to inspect the work and certify that the pilings were being correctly installed. Expertise, supervision, verification. Ha. Try fraud, incompetency, and conspiracy.

No one had been doing their job correctly and now no one was the least bit interested in being held accountable for it.

Bottom line: we were going to have to test every piling to see if they went to bedrock and then, if they didn't, we would need to redesign the foundation with another piling design that did go to bedrock and remove all seven feet of cement that Plumb Level & Square had poured over the grade beams to hide their fraud. All of this while we're scrambling to get the stop-work order lifted.

As I said, a smart man would have stopped there.

I have never been accused of being a smart man.

Things soon went from horrible to abysmal...

CHAPTER THREE

WE ARE BUILDERS

❝*A common mistake that people make when trying to design something completely foolproof is to underestimate the ingenuity of complete fools.*

Douglas Adams

Four years earlier...

The year 2002 was to be a major turning point for our young family. Pam and I were thrilled because this would be our first year living outside of a construction site since we were married in 1996. We'd bought 121 West 15th Street (our first building together) four months after our wedding in New Orleans. Neither of us were native New Yorkers, but we'd both fallen in love with the neighborhood and decided to build our life together here. Renovating this building was the anchor piece to our dreams. Now it was finally drawing to a conclusion. For the first time in six years, we would be living dust-free, with privacy, four solid walls, no contractors to supervise, access to all our possessions (including our wedding presents, which we were finally able to unpack), clean clothes, and best of all, running water, a refrigerator, a washer and dryer, and a stove all our own to cook on. Actually cook—after six years of living on take-out. Which actually isn't that terrible in a city that always has multiple restaurants open 24/7. Finally, we would be living together as a regular family. (The property at 121 West 15th street can be viewed on www.TerrapinDesign.net.)

You've heard of the boy in the bubble. Pam and I were the couple in the bubble. Plastic-lined, makeshift rooms had been our chief residence during the six years in which we oversaw the renovation. We'd bought the place at a "steal" for just over $900,000 (I believe it was the last Manhattan brownstone to sell for under a million), and completely rebuilt and redesigned it, installing brand new electric and plumbing systems as well as a host of custom touches. During the construction years we lived almost solely in "dust-reduced" (not dust-free) bubble rooms. Every now and then, when the building became totally unlivable or our nerves became frazzled beyond belief, we'd escape to a transient offsite habitation to keep our sanity. But mostly we were the couple in the bubble.

Some of our bubble rooms weren't too bad and in the beginning some of them even had amenities, but typically they were without running water or sanitation. Invariably they involved a plastic sheet divider between our living area and the construction site. Held together by duct tape and staples. It was our feeble attempt to keep the dust out and to live in a semi-civilized fashion. Feeble is the operant word here: the rooms were usually large enough for only our bed and dressers, roughly 8 x 10 feet. Tight even by Manhattan standards. Basically the size of a one-person SRO. They provided room for us to sleep and dress. Th-th-th-that's all, folks.

That was our living situation for six years. No cooking, bathing, or relaxing at home. Our lives consisted of working on the building, commuting to and from our jobs, eating out, and sleeping. We were totally immersed in the design work and the management of the sub-contractors while also working full-time to pay for it all. With the interest we were paying for the financing, we had to keep things moving briskly along.

Living in a gutted home without running water is like traveling & camping constantly, except you never go anywhere. We carried our toiletries with us at all times in case we happened on an opportunity to take a shower. Many a time we showed up early at friends' dinner parties not only to help them set up, but also to shower. The building wasn't so bad in the spring or fall, but winter and summer were awful, without AC or heat. When circumstances forced us out of our bubble rooms we lived like gypsies. During the last two years of construction we spent time in a couple of especially colorful offsite abodes...

At one point we lived for six months on our Hunter 34-foot sailboat Jouer at Chelsea Piers with our two cats Sunrise and Sunset. Living on a boat with pets is a trip in itself, but living on a boat with pets in one of the busiest harbors in the world, on a river with a rip tide, is another story altogether. First of all, you have to get used to constant motion. And I do mean constant. The water never sits still, but moves in complicated, unpredictable patterns. That wasn't a problem for me but Pam was on a steady diet of Dramamine for six months. The Hudson River is a commercial river, which means lots of tugboats. Chelsea Piers Marina has no break wall so the rollers made by the tugs hit you full on. The tugs' wakes start coming in at 4 a.m. The best part is that after a wave hits you, it goes another 50 feet and then rebounds off the banks of Manhattan and whacks you again on the way out. A twofer special! So you spend 4 a.m. to 7 a.m. each morning in what you could politely call "choppy seas," getting jerked around at the end of your dock line like a mackerel jig. We went through two sets of dock lines a season at that marina due to wear and tear.

Dockside living created a particularly daunting challenge for our cats. Sunrise and Sunset loved roaming the docks and meeting all the people. Jumping off the boat was easy. Getting back on was another game. The kitties could not gauge whether a wave was coming towards the boat or away from it. They would jump for the boat, but if a wave hit at the same time, they would meet the rising boat in midair, smack into the side of it and slide into the river. As everyone knows, cats and H2O are not a happy mix. As soon as they'd hit the water, the Hudson River tide, which runs at about five knots, would suck them in. The docks at Chelsea Piers were lined with plastic so the cats couldn't grab onto anything until they were swept another twenty feet further along and under the piers for the golf driving range, which were made of wood. There they could use their claws to dig into the wood and cling on for dear life until the cavalry arrived.

Several times we came home from work to hear an incredibly loud meowing coming from under the piers next to the marina. It would be Sunrise screaming bloody murder. Who knew how many hours she'd been stuck there. I would have to put on a wetsuit and jump in after her. She would claw into my shoulders and ride back to the dock on top of me. Sunrise definitely used up a few of her nine lives that summer at the marina. My wetsuit didn't have a whole lot of resale value after that, as I recall.

We also sublet a studio in the Meatpacking District for the last fall of our construction. This place was so bad I had to paint it from top to bottom before I'd even allow one box of our belongings to cross its threshold. The previous tenant chain-smoked and the place was non-ventilated. The walls were covered with enough brown tar to seal a driveway. It took three coats of the best white paint to cover it and get rid of the smell. It was the only place available in the area at a reasonable price. We took it knowing we'd both be working long hours, so all we needed was a place for our cats and our beds, and to have—miracle of miracles—an actual bathroom with running water. One of the studio's feature attractions was that you had to leave the bathroom light on and the bathroom door open 24/7 in a vain attempt to avoid being overrun by roaches. But as far as I could tell, the bugs still managed to run a fairly successful dry-cleaning business from under the sink.

The place was on the first floor of a SRO building with its sole window offering a lovely view of the garbage cans on the street. The Meatpacking District had not been completely gentrified at that time. There were still meat distributors and butchers in many of its buildings, and blood all over its sidewalks every morning. On a hot August day, wow—stench is too kind a word. Each morning trucks would drop off whole sides of beef and every meat product imaginable (along with a few that were pretty unimaginable) for distribution throughout the city. What a sight. Raw meat hanging on rails of hooks all over the sidewalks; men in bloody white coats hauling carcasses off trucks; hung-over minimum-wage workers hosing ropy entrails off sidewalks. That was the scene. Day after day.

After the trucks would back up to the loading dock in the early morning, the drivers had a few hours to kill. Which made them handy customers for the world's oldest profession. More than once during our rental, I had to kick streetwalkers performing "cranial ministrations" off the hood of my car so

I could drive to work. Sometimes I'd have to lean on the horn for several seconds or actually move the car in order to break their concentration. They would grudgingly schlep to the next car's hood and get back to business before I even pulled away. If there is a sight on Earth more depressing than the stubble on the face of a heavily rouged, 49-year-old, cross-dressing hooker as s/he goes down on a fat trucker in the six a.m. light of the Meatpacking District, then I don't know what it is. Pam and I both worked long hours that fall and spent as little "awake time" as possible in and around that sublet. Wonder why.

We moved back to our gutted condo at 121 West 15th Street in January, 1999, and lived there for a while with no rear wall to the building. Man, what a winter! The entire back of the building was exposed to the elements with only plastic sheets keeping out the rain and snow. We made a small bubble room on the first floor that housed our bed and clothes. Fortunately the furnace was on the bottom floor. Its heat plus a few space heaters kept us in some semblance of warmth. Not walk-around-naked warmth, but at least coffee-remains-in-liquid-state-for-a-few-hours warmth. We could see our breath when we said our good-mornings.

Our bathroom at that time was the McDonald's on 6th & 14th Street, our shower was the YMCA on 14th Street (the actual YMCA the Village People sang about, relocated from its original site on 23rd St.), and our kitchen was an endless stream of New York City restaurants and take-out joints. One high point was New Year's Eve, 1999. Because everyone was going crazy about the end of the world—remember the whole Y2K thing, where all the computers were going to be wiped clean, destroying the banking system (no such luck) and life as we knew it?—we decided to have a Black Tie catered New Year's Eve Party in our raw, unfinished space. Everyone had to bring something significant from the twentieth century to put in a time capsule, which we later cemented in our bedroom fireplace along with a commemorative plaque. We got a lot of great items—a New York Times from the date of the first moon-walk, a David Bowie vinyl album and some original Grateful Dead bootlegs, Silly Putty, art signed by local artists, and much more. It was a fun night for twelve couples and a great way to christen our new digs before they were finished.

#

Pam was indispensable during the whole renovation. You never know how your relationship is going to weather life's storms until you actually put it to the test. Boy, did I luck out with Pam. She is a non-conformist like me with a big rebel heart, proud native Kentuckian. Her mother and grandmother were both Daughters of the American Revolution. No matter what, Pam stands by what she believes in. This should have been no surprise to me, considering the way she'd hung in there with me during my "personal renovation" project a few years earlier. Within a year of being married, there'd been an alcohol stove accident on our sailboat in which I suffered 3rd degree burns over thirty percent of my upper body and nearly died. It was Labor Day, 1996, and we were hanging out with friends on our boat off Oyster Bay, Long Island. I went below deck to tend to something on the stove and kaflooey. Alcohol fumes ignited, and I was a man on fire.

I ended up spending weeks in the hospital, as you can imagine. Twenty-eight days on morphine. My own mother didn't even recognize me the first time she visited. The treatments were heinous. Have you ever heard Richard Pryor describing his burn treatments? It's pretty accurate. They use these incredibly soft towels to wash the burns, but they feel like barbed wire. They give you just enough morphine to take the edge off the pain, but they can't give you too much, because you have to feel it so they can know if they're causing damage. (I actually did a lot of the design work on 121 West 15th Street while on morphine in the hospital, which might help explain a few of our more "creative" choices.)

I ended up having thirteen skin grafts and had to wear a special skin suit for a year. I looked like Omega Man. It couldn't have been easy for Pam to see her newlywed husband in that kind of shape. But she stayed by my side the whole time, never showing her own fear or discomfort. She was my rock.

If she could tough that one out, then I guess a building renovation was small potatoes.

The workmen called her a saint for putting up with the mess for so long. She was a total trouper, never complaining (okay, rarely complaining) about the disgusting condition of the toilets at the McDonald's or the lack of privacy and security in our bubble rooms. She put up with an endless barrage of indignities and handled it all with grace and good spirits. Every once in a while, we'd take a vacation weekend at a local hotel in Chelsea just to feel human again. Boy would we rock those amenities! This would recharge our batteries just enough to persevere through another six months of construction. We'd also go on extended breaks for the holidays. Like normal people, to regroup.

Pam was the face of the day-to-day operation. She would meet the contractors at breakfast every morning and dole out instructions and changes. The contractors became members of the family. They celebrated birthdays, anniversaries, and weekend barbecues with us.

Pam also designed a lot of the interior details for our home, as well as all of the color coordination and color schemes for the building. She has a great eye for composition and a creative mind when it comes to living spaces. A few of the more unique details in our home condo:

- A two-story stone waterfall that flows continuously over a working fireplace and empties into…

- A scale replica of the Yangtze River that cuts across the entire lower-level living room and functions as a circulated koi pond covered in Plexiglas

- A steel and blue-glass staircase, designed to look like flowing water, lit from within

- An entire room wallpapered in laminated pages from the classic comic books Asterix and Obelix, in a collage

- A replica of Van Gogh's Starry Night, fashioned out of thousands of translucent, colored marbles set in a suspended ceiling grid and lit from above

- Countertops and tabletops made from bowling alley wood

- Custom cement countertops in the kitchen

- A built-in luxury "tree house" for kids overlooking an outdoor redwood hot tub in the back yard

- Solid brass fire pole installed for quick access in rear of apartment

More of www.TerrapinDesign.net

And that was just for our condo. There were also the upstairs condos, which we would later sell and which were sometimes rented out for high-end photo shoots, such as a memorable one for Playgirl magazine.

By the time our daughter Breana was born in 2001, though, we were eager to stop building our condo and start building our family.

We finally got our home completed in 2002 and breathed a gigantic sigh of relief. Now it was time to sit back and enjoy what we had created. Time to become a "normal" everyday couple with a newborn. Which, as any new parent can attest, is anything but normal. You know the drill: no sleep, no uninterrupted mealtimes, no intimate time together as a couple. But we relished it. At least we were doing it together in a real home. This was truly a turning point in our life together. All our hard work had produced something truly satisfying and uniquely our own. The waterfall produced a lovely trickling sound that could be heard throughout the house. The koi in our miniature Yangtze loved swimming outdoors and in again through the connecting tunnel. We had built an oasis of tranquility with a natural feel right in the middle of Manhattan. We could now focus on expanding the Rath clan, building some financial security, and making our space into a real home.

But as a lifelong fan of the Grateful Dead, I was soon reminded of Mr. Jerry Garcia's classic song lyric, "When life looks like easy street, there is danger at your door." Our time of domestic tranquility was not destined to last…

CHAPTER FOUR

IT ALL BEGINS WITH A LAWSUIT
(THIS IS MANHATTAN, AFTER ALL)

> **❝***Twenty years from now you will be more
> disappointed by the things you didn't do
> than by the ones you did do. So throw off
> the bowlines. Sail away from the safe harbor.
> Catch the trade winds in your sails. Explore.
> Dream. Discover.*
>
> Mark Twain

One goes through many rites of passage when becoming a New Yorker or, more specifically, a Manhattanite. I was from Connecticut and Pam was from Kentucky. Although we both felt more at home in the city than anywhere else on Earth, it still took years of hands-on education for us to become true natives. Pam had had a head start living in the Upper West Side for eighteen years before we met, but I was a novice.

As time passes you slowly acquire gems of local knowledge that make living in Manhattan slightly easier and more efficient. Some are little tips that lessen the effects of all the congestion. Like learning the alternate-side-of-the-street parking rules, finding all the "hidden" parking spots where you won't get ticketed, or getting to know the intricacies of the city's traffic patterns so you can school a cab driver on a quicker/cheaper route to your destination across town. Others are basic necessities like learning to navigate the subway system without a map so you don't waste all your time and money in cabs. Then there are the consumer lessons you learn like finding all the little hole-in-the-wall places where the best of every kind of ethnic food can be bought, along with the sometimes-weird rituals for obtaining same. (That bit about the Soup Nazi on Seinfeld was only a slight exaggeration.)

Others rites of passage include learning certain lessons the hard way. A lot of these involve street merchant frauds and grifter cons. For example: someone's standing outside the door to an apartment and asks for money because he just locked himself out and needs cab fare to get the spare set of keys, or asks for gas money in a gas station even though he doesn't seem to have a car. Or my personal favorite, the frantic set designer's assistant who is late for an opening-night show and needs cab money right away to retrieve an important set piece so the show can go on. Then, of course, there are those "designer" purses for sale on every corner with misspelled famous designer names. Enough said. Learning these lessons are just a few of the many rites of Manhattanization.

There's another Manhattan rite of passage I was hoping to avoid: the lawsuit. Every landowner in Manhattan eventually gets sued. It's almost a coming-of-age requirement. Once you've turned 40 and you own property, you will get sued; I'd heard this many times, usually from other property owners who wore their past lawsuits like badges of honor. Well, I had just turned 40 and was starting to look over my shoulder. When would it happen to me?

Fittingly enough for a Manhattan tale, it was indeed a lawsuit that would set in motion the chain of events that eventually led to the fateful rockslide in 2006, which then led to my tumbling into more debt than I could pay off in five lifetimes, irreparable problems with my siblings, and foreclosure on the home I and my family loved.

Ah well, it is what it is.

That expression, by the way—"it is what it is"—became like a mantra; one that Pam and I heard over and over again from the mouths of attorneys, contractors, bankers, bureaucrats and just about everyone else we dealt with during our adventure in real estate. I guess it's something Manhattanites say whenever a fellow human being is naïve enough to express incredulity over some act of corruption, ineptitude, or outright thievery in the City That Never Sleeps. "It is what it is." It's another way of saying, "Grow up, deal with it, this is how things are." Personally, I've always hated the expression. To me, it's like rolling over and accepting the reprehensible as normal. A couple of years ago, though, I heard the same words coming out of my own mouth. That was the day I started writing this book.

Anyway, back to the nasty "L" word. Lawsuit.

When Pam and I bought the first brownstone in 1996, it was not only going to be our home, but our first real estate development project. The plan was to keep one of the condos for ourselves and sell the others. We couldn't afford to buy the building on our own, so we partnered with a "junior owner," a friend of Pam's named Jim Sandino.

Pam befriended Jim during her modeling days. He was quite the playboy back them (He always enjoyed telling his story of dating four Kelly's who were flight attendants on different airlines back in the day) , but now he was settling down with his girlfriend Serina (20 years his junior), getting married again. Jim had a successful pharmaceutical marketing business and decided it was time to acquire some assets. Like a trophy wife (she got a boob job for Christmas that year) and brownstone address. Jim with his dark hair & pin stripe business suit epitomized another NYC rule: Don't believe what any New Yorker says at a cocktail party or out at night because by the light of day 9 out of 10 times its false or so exaggerated it usually is not worth following up on. He was a great guy, a lot of fun to be with and had a good heart. But, he just got caught up into exaggerations. Usually harmless. We narrowed down our possibilities and came up with Jim as the best possibility. He was going to be one of the condo owners and was willing to put up some money on the building. As junior owner he had 40% ownership of the whole property. His name was not on the mortgage or title, nor was he expected to do any of the management, renovation, rehabilitation, design, or maintenance on anything in the building outside his condo. That was to be Pam's and my thing. Jim signed a series of agreements to this effect when we purchased the building in1996. That was all ok with Jim at the time. But, as we all know time doesn't stay still.

By September 2002, though, Mr. Jim Sandino had been growing increasingly testy about our business relationship; particularly the management of the building and finances. He had seen the building increase steadily in value over the years as the renovation went on, and felt that he should get some of the fruits of the labor Pam and I had been putting into it. If you'll recall, 2002 was the start of the final run of the housing boom. The building had indeed appreciated well, but Pam and I had put a lot of money and time into the renovation also. So there was equity, yes, but if you calculated in the substantial costs of the renovations, the profit wasn't as large as it would seem at first blush. This was a concept that Jim couldn't seem to fathom.

At the time, Jim was trying to expand his pharmaceutical marketing business and was in need of financing. He figured that pulling equity out of the building would be a good place to grab some fast capital. The problem was that his name wasn't on the title or mortgage so he couldn't borrow against it. Not from the bank, anyway. See, the building was bought in my name because at the time of the purchase, in 1996, Mr. Sandino didn't have any credit or equity. He actually borrowed the $100,000 from multiple friends to put money into the building. It actually was an eleventh hour scramble for Jim. But, to his credit he did get it done.

That meant in order for him to borrow against his share of the equity, I would have to take out the loan personally, then turn around and hand the money to him. At which point, of course, I, not Jim, would be legally liable for his loan. Things were on shaky ground between us already, and Jim had already amassed a list of grievances against me. So I didn't feel comfortable giving him a personal loan. I figured once he was holding my cash, he would come up with all kinds of rationalizations for not paying me back. Add to that the fact that Mr. Sandino was not well known for paying his bills on time. It seemed pretty clear to me that if I lent him money it would be only a matter of time before his problems came back to haunt me. I couldn't afford that right now. Bottom line: I refused to allow him to take a loan out on the building.

Things quickly went from bad to worse between us. We held a series of "emergency" meetings in various neighborhood restaurants trying to iron out our problems and avert disaster. These meetings would typically need to be rescheduled four or five times because of Jim's busy schedule. We'd end up cramming down some food and talking between bites for thirty minutes, trying to resolve a very complex and sensitive situation. Needless to say, after three months of such pow-wows nothing much was accomplished. In addition, I began to hear more and more grumblings about how his wife wanted to get out of New York, so I figured the writing was already on the wall. Jim wanted out. All that remained was for him to pull the trigger.

He finally did so. He gave us notice that he wanted to terminate the contract for his ownership of the building. Fine. Our agreement gave either partner the right to request a termination. If this right were exercised, the other partner had first right of refusal to purchase the exiting partner's ownership. The price of that ownership could be set by mutual agreement or by an independently assigned value as determined by a neutral appraiser.

One might think this would be easy. Hire an appraiser, determine the value of the property, and then calculate the appreciation (profit) to date. Well, in fact, the appraisal part did go fairly smoothly—we were both in general agreement as to the current value of the property—but determining the profit? That was another world for Mr. Sandino. He seemed upset that I insisted on relying on an arcane system known as math to make my calculations. The situation seemed pretty clear to me. I had been paying for 60% of all the renovation costs because I owned 60% of the building. Since I had paid a larger percentage of the renovation costs, I, by definition, had invested more money in the building. I kept detailed accounting records on all those investments, along with Mr. Sandino's contributions. Annual tax returns were filed on the building, with both of our expenditures clearly declared so that when the building sold, our capital gains would be less.

Profit is defined as selling price minus costs. You add up all the money you've spent to produce a product or service and get it to market, you subtract those costs from the selling price, and that's your profit. Thus has the concept of profit been defined in Business 101 in schools across the world since the first business course was taught.

In our case, profit would be the appraised market value of the building minus all of the renovation costs, minus the outstanding original mortgage. Then you would take 40% of that amount—representing Mr. Sandino's share of the ownership—and that would be the buyout price for his ownership. Correct?

Well, that math did not sit well with Jim. His idea was appraised price = profit. Period. He believed he should be paid 40% of the pure increase in value. I told him I could not agree to that formula because, well, it was insane. Two days after we reached a verbal impasse, Jim served us notice for a lawsuit. So obviously he'd already had a lawyer working on it for a while. To think, I'd been a groomsman at this guy's wedding. (In the spirit of full disclosure, it was his third wedding and to a trophy wife. But still…) Now our relationship was going to end over money. Shocking in Manhattan, right?

Oh well, it is what it is.

Lawsuits are always about money. People may tell you they're about principles, about justice, about righting wrongs, about protecting the innocent, but they're always about money, at least when it comes to real estate. Always.

The resulting dilemma was twofold for Pam and me. First, we had to negotiate a settlement to buy Sandino out. Given the fact that he and I had very different ideas about what the word profit meant, this would take some time. But what typically happens in a case like this is that, over a course of many months (sometimes years) and many carefully worded phone calls, letters, and emails from lawyers, you gradually move closer, till you finally hit on a figure you can both live with. Settling out of court is always the best course of action, because once you take matters into a courtroom, all of the money ends up in your lawyers' boats. So I figured it would be a matter of time until we both moved closer together on price (which eventually did happen).

The second, and trickier part, was that Pam and I had to obtain the funds to actually pay for the buyout without going broke in the process. We had some money saved but money goes quickly in Manhattan, especially with kids.

Actually, it was the "kids" part that got us thinking about solving our money dilemma in a bigger way. We could already see that we needed more room for our daughter Breana. She was now 4 and growing like a bamboo plant on Miracle-Gro. Plus, we had decided to have more children and that process was already out of the gate. Pam had started in vitro fertilization and I was giving her shots daily for it. And, that had the possible outcome of having up to 6 additions to the family. Financially, we were pretty comfortable in those days. If the lawsuit had not happened, we might have been able to continue on the course of action we were already on—enjoying our new life of relative plenty with four walls and home-cooked meals. But the need for a massive influx of capital sort of made that plan obsolete. Maybe that wasn't such a bad thing. Maybe—we started to think—we ought to find a bigger, better solution that would not only solve the Jim problem, but would also benefit our family in the long run. To be honest, it was not in my nature to sit still anyway. Now that the building at 121 West 15th Street was finished, I began itching for a new project. I didn't want to just get out from under the Jim problem, I wanted to build a better future for us. I was still young and full of ambition, piss, and vinegar.

When I took an honest look at our life, I knew that all of our apparent "prosperity" was built on a financial house of cards, one that required round-the-clock maintenance to keep standing. And that worried me.

I had already refinanced the renovation of our building several times over. Back then refinancing was not a problem for a homeowner. You could use your own appraiser and the banks were begging to give money away. You would apply for a loan and the banks would offer more than you asked for. "No, go ahead, take it"; like it was the leftover slice of pizza. The Loan to Value went from 70% to 90%. Meaning you had to put less and less money down, and some banks were only requiring 5%. The financing fees were relatively negligible and could be written off against your income taxes.

I was getting ten phone calls a week for refinancing, not to mention all the mail, radio, and television ads. Banks were on a lending craze. Why not? They were assuming virtually no risk. The bank would just dump your loan on a third party the same day you signed the mortgage. Typically the banks wouldn't even sign your loan until they had already sold it in the secondary market. I remember, in fact, once waiting for two weeks for Countrywide Mortgage to close my loan because they hadn't sold it yet. So how did these guys make money if they didn't hold the loans? Mortgage brokers got commissions and banks got bonuses. It beat taking risks. The bank immediately passed the risk of any loan they approved onto a finance corporation that bought and bundled these mortgages. The bundles were then traded away, over and over, until someone on the other side of the world got stuck with them. Who actually owned any given property at any given time became a matter of legitimate debate. Once your mortgage was sold in the secondary market it became next to impossible to identify who actually owned it. We're talking about houses of cards built on other houses of cards. The real estate market finance was going gangbusters because the banks literally had nothing to lose! They passed all the risk on to the secondary market.

So… the solution was to finance my way out of this buyout. And maybe, when the construction dust settled, eventually end up with something real that my family could use to build some wealth on.

The problem was, I was leveraged to the hilt. I needed another equity source so that I could manage my way out of this debt. Another building project to develop would satisfy those financial needs. I could then finance my way through the development and sell the resulting condos to pay my way out of this debt and live in one of the condos mortgage free in Manhattan.

All I needed was another asset to leverage...

CHAPTER FIVE

LOCATION, LOCATION, LOCATION

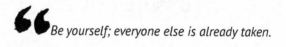

Be yourself; everyone else is already taken.

Oscar Wilde

We spent over a year looking for a new place that fit our needs. There were several criteria the building needed to fill. From an investment/financial perspective, it had to be an undervalued property—a major "fixer upper" for sure—with strong development potential, so that we could convert it into high-end condos to sell. It also needed to have good re-fi value a year or two down the road without much investment. On a practical level, it needed to be a place that would give our growing family more living space, in a reasonably safe neighborhood that appealed to us. Oh, and parking. It had to have parking, or at least potential to build that in. For the past seven years I'd been paying $450 a month for off-street parking and I was over it. Big time. The rest of our family's needs could be handled by designing them into the new space.

We went through several potential deals that fell apart for one reason or another, from misrepresentations of property income to good old-fashioned scamming and mental insanity (never too far below the surface in New York). We came very close to one purchase, but then the guy started whispering to me about wanting to keep some of the money off the books—I think he was going through a nasty divorce or something. When he asked me to meet him in an alley with $150,000 in cash in a paper bag—true story—I decided maybe this wasn't the right deal for us after all.

When we finally learned that 123 West 15th Street—the building right next door to ours—was on the market, Pam and I felt a quiet rush of excitement.

Perhaps destiny had orchestrated all those broken deals so that the timing would work out for us to purchase it, just like the woman in a romantic comedy who has to date seven losers in order to meet Mr. Right at the perfect moment.

If we were going to buy another building—and that was still a big if—it seemed we couldn't do better than this one. The top three reasons 123 West 15th made immediate sense to us? The standards: location, location, location. The building was literally touching ours. We shared a common partition with it (which, unfortunately, had necessitated a lawsuit with the current owner over a sagging outer wall some years earlier). There literally wasn't a property in all of the five boroughs that made more sense to own from a location perspective.

For starters, we could combine our current condo with the bottom two floors on the new place, which would double our living space and give us a "double wide" back yard for the kids (40 by 50 feet-plus, a very big yard for Manhattan). Pam got a kick out of using the phrase "double wide" to describe our Chelsea apartment expansion. Back home in her native Kentucky, the term refers, of course, to double-wide trailers. Because so many people live in single trailers in the Kentucky hills, owning a double-wide was something of a status symbol. So Pam immediately glommed onto the concept (mostly in a tongue-in-cheek way, but I think it worked on a primal level too). As a bonus, the doubled street frontage would allow us to put in a curb cut for a garage. Parking problem solved. We checked with our expeditor Andy and the Department of Buildings and found out that all this was all doable. Theoretically.

But we were still far from certain we wanted to do this.

Though the place at 123 West 15th Street was ideal in many ways, and really got our design juices flowing, there were some major buts. First of all, the investment was going to be huge and risky. We were in the middle of a lawsuit with Sandino, which was strapping us money-wise. Even though we'd be borrowing most of the money, if it all went south, we'd be left holding the bag. A very large one at that. Secondly, and this was a bigger issue, deep in our bones we were tired of dealing with construction headaches. We'd just gone through six years of living in renovation at 121 West 15th Street. We wanted to enjoy our lives for a change.

In fact, it went beyond that; we were having major cruising dreams. We talked often about wanting to free ourselves from the moorings of real estate and sail off into the sunset. Both Pam and I loved sailing more than anything else in the world. Sailing, when you think about it, is just about the polar opposite of real estate development. It's all about casting free rather than securing down. Water versus earth. These ocean voyage dreams of ours weren't just empty fantasies, either. We were growing more and more serious about the idea of spending a few years aboard the boat and exploring the world.

So the ocean was pulling at our hearts, while our heads were shopping for a building. Something wasn't stacking up here. Did we really want to anchor ourselves to another several years of construction and drywall dust when our hearts were craving the taste of sea spray in our faces?

There were some major drawbacks to the property as well. Chief among them: 123 West 15th Street was a Single Room Occupancy building. It was comprised of seventeen rent-regulated SRO rooms. That's a big red flag. Rent control in New York City is a quagmire—a boon for tenants, but an absolute nightmare for building owners. Not only are you forbidden from charging market-value rents that make your investment and expenditures financially worthwhile, but virtually all of the regulations concerning rent payments/non-payments, evictions, rate increases, disputes, utilities, and repairs are slanted heavily in the pro-tenant direction. In New York City, landlords are considered pure evil.

So you'd have to be crazy to go near a rent-regulated building, right? Normally, yes, but here's the thing: we wouldn't be buying it as a going concern. Our intention would be to phase out the current tenants by attrition as we renovated. The great thing about 123 West 15th Street—its saving grace, really—was that only nine tenants were living in the building at the time. Nearly half the seventeen units were empty. This was a huge advantage to a new owner/developer. It meant the current tenants could be housed on the upper floors while we worked on the lower floors, and eventually those tenants would move out, of their own accord, or, not to put too fine a point on it, decease. And given the health status of some of the residents, hospitalization or the latter was a distinct possibility for a few. Not to be insensitive, but you had to look at this objectively from an investment perspective.

So maybe we could handle the tenant situation. Maybe.

It really came down to a choice: did we really want to do this? Make a huge time and money commitment to a new property just when we were starting to enjoy the perks of living without construction headaches? And when our hearts were being pulled toward the seven seas?

Well, the "pros" list was pretty damn compelling…

First and foremost, the purchase would give us the means to resolve the Jim Sandino dilemma. I didn't have enough cash on hand to pay him off, but I did have enough to put a down payment on a building, and back in those days I had great credit. (Today I can't finance a bag of peanuts, but we'll get into that later.) Remember, this was 2003-2004. Every major bank was giving mortgages away, and closings happened in 45 days. You could provide your own appraisal—I think you could pretty much scribble comps on a cocktail napkin—and the bank would usually approve it. Manhattan real estate was going ape-shit and no one thought the market would ever slow down. By combining my building at 121 West 15th Street with 123 West 15th Street I would have two substantial real estate assets to refinance. The banks were hungry for jumbo loans to package together and sell in the secondary market. These loans were all at reasonable rates of 5.75% at the time. The banks were just keeping the commission machine going and providing more bundles to the secondary market. (The world will never see a credit market like that again.)

Refinancing would be the key. We'd need to refinance the two-building combo once it had gained some value. As I said before, refinancing was not new to us. We had refinanced 121 West 15th Street five times between 1996 and 2004 and the appraised value for the building went from $1,000,000 to $5,000,000. The interest rates remained stable or lower, with better terms, each mortgage we refinanced. So it seemed entirely feasible that we could pull enough money out of the twin properties to pay Sandino off in the near future. With more than a little left over to seed our renovation project.

From a family perspective, the place was a no-brainer. This new building would allow us to double our living space and our play space, without having to move away from a neighborhood and schools we loved.

We could create our own off-street parking, too. Enough said.

From a development/construction point of view, the building had what we needed. It was in pretty rough shape, which was what we were looking for. That would presumably keep the price affordable, and, since we would be doing extensive renovations, we didn't care about its condition as long as the underlying structure was sound. Space-wise, there was plenty of room to not only create our own huge living quarters, but also to carve out several luxury condos that we could sell to recoup our investment and build ourselves a nice nest egg.

The really ideal part was that we could supervise all of the construction, up close and personal, without needing to live in it—all the advantages of living on site, without the bubble living. We could deal with the contractors all day long, then walk next-door to our clean, comfortable, dust-free home, sit with the koi, and enjoy our oasis in the city.

All of those reasons were good ones, but, if I was being honest, there was an even bigger pull for me.

I needed a challenge in my life. I was getting antsy. I had just spent six years restoring a brownstone inside and out. It had come out great and was one of the best business decisions I'd ever made. I was discovering that I was pretty good at real estate development. I was itching to put what I'd learned on 121 West 15th Street to good use and to build something even bigger and better than the original project. The market was ripe for green development and there were some exciting new green technologies hitting the market that were virtually untried in Manhattan. There was a possibility of creating something truly groundbreaking and attention-getting here.

The fact was, my day job at Better Lists Inc. was not particularly challenging and didn't provide the creative satisfaction I craved. Running a direct mail fulfillment company came down to just selling a generic commodity/service. "Success" in the business was only a matter of selling more printing jobs or doing more pick-and-pack projects for more companies. Kicking up the numbers. It was paperclip and cookie-cutter kind of work—no inner satisfaction other than the profits it provided. Direct Mail can be a real cash cow in good times, but the industry is constantly changing and being redefined by the internet. Printing and fulfillment has devolved into a commodity defined only by price. I needed to make a substantive career move to secure my family's future and I wanted to do it creatively.

In truth, my ego had needs too. I longed to get some recognition for my creativity. I wanted to make a building that would get noticed in the crowded market of Manhattan. I wanted to make some waves. (Be careful what you wish for, as they say.)

Hubris would turn out to be my downfall, one could argue. But then again, without hubris I wouldn't have gotten through the construction of 121 West 15th, learned how to successfully race sailboats, or accomplished some of the most memorable achievements of my life.

By nature I'm a risk taker. When I decide I want something, I don't soft-shoe around it. I dive in and then learn as I go. Some years earlier, for example, I decided I wanted to be a futures commodity bond trader. I didn't go back to school and "get my degree" or work my way up. Instead, I gave myself a crash course in investment strategies, got my Series 7 license to practice as a stockbroker, borrowed money against my house, threw together $150,000 in cash, and headed out to Chicago to try my hand on the Board of Trade. I worked as a runner for six weeks, to learn the practical ropes, took every class the Board gave on trading, then bought myself a seat on the trading floor and started trading with my own money.

As a trader, I was always pushing a position to the max if I believed in it, and often taking some heat on it. "Taking heat" means losing money, at least temporarily, during the day trading session. But if I believed it was a good position, I didn't run away from it. I kept it and added to it. And more often than not it paid off big in the end. I learned how to handle the pressure and how to control my edge.

"If you're not living on the edge, you're taking up too much room," a fellow sailor, Jim Bishop, was known to say. One of my favorite books is Reminiscences of a Stock Operator, which should tell you a bit about my character. It's a biography of a stock operator (stock trader in the 1930's) amassing fortunes and losing them several times over in the market. The one thing I have always said is that I will never look back on my life and wish I had done something I truly desired to do. No regrets. Ever.

I ended up spending three years as a trader, screaming at the top of my lungs in the pit every day and trading $5 million to $30 million on a daily basis, getting in and out of positions, scalping. It was an exciting life, best job I ever had. So that's one side of my "hubris"; a side I'd never want to live without.

The flip side? Well, I got blown out as a trader on the second night of the First Gulf War. I was on the wrong side when the first scuds flew into Israel. See, the first night of the war the Air Force went in and it looked like we'd blasted

Saddam back to the Stone Age. It seemed this war would be a cakewalk. I went into the night trading floor with a great position and got on the right side of the war from the start. I had four points into my position before the close and I reduced my position and got out, happy with the six figure profit on the trade. Next day, the market went up a little more and wavered back and forth. So I started to build up a position again with some profit in it, trading in and out all day. The second night, the pit was full of traders because everyone had seen the frenzy the night before. As the bombing continued in Iraq, the market continued to react positively.

Then, suddenly, the first scuds came flying into Israel and the market stopped on a dime and threw itself into reverse. Talk was, there might be gas or other nasty stuff in the scuds. This cakewalk might turn into World War III. The market dropped six points in a blink of an eye and everyone was selling. No one was buying. I was not a big trader, but I did trade large positions every once in a while and today was one of those days. By the time I got out of that one I had a call on my voicemail to meet with the brokerage house clearer the next day. I couldn't cover my trades. My seat on the on the exchange was sold and I was finished.

A couple of weeks later I found myself driving east on Route 80 in a rented truck with all my possessions—not much, a Honda 750 my brother had given me, some clothes packed in Glad trash bags, and a couple boxes of photographs. That was all I had to show for three years of trading bonds as an independent on the MidAm at the Board of Trade in Chicago.

Did I regret my decision, though? Not one bit. Lots of people play it safe their whole lives, only to have family, financial, or health problems derail their dreams before they realize them in the end. I feel you have only one crack at this life. Live today to the max because you have no idea what the tide will bring in tomorrow. Or if there'll even be a tomorrow for you.

Fast-forward to 2003. Here I was, itching to roll the dice again. On a huge real estate play. But this time things were different. I had a family. Did I have a right to risk their security for the sake of my ambitions? The truth was, we didn't really need to do this deal. If we played things conservatively we could refinance our current building again, pay off my ex-partner slowly, continue to live in our not-quite-big-enough space, and coast by, making payments on 121 West 15th Street. Then thirty years down the road we'd probably have some security. Maybe that was the more responsible course of action. But sorry, that's not me. Sometimes I wish it was. Life would be a hell of a lot easier.

To complicate matters even more, there was the head vs. heart issue I've already mentioned. My head, my ego, wanted to create a name for myself and build the coolest building in Manhattan. Make some money. Get some publicity. Impress some newspaper and magazine writers. But in my heart and soul I was beginning to recoil against that very mindset. Pam and I were growing wearier by the day of the value system of popular American culture. We both felt that America was becoming a place we didn't recognize and didn't like very much anymore. We felt the country's values were changing rapidly for the worse. The new value system seemed to be "as long as you make money or get famous, anything goes." Business ethics no longer existed, except as a marketing gimmick. No one seemed to care anymore about working hard, creating value, being true to your word, and making the world a better place for those around you. Materialism was quickly becoming the one and only real religion—wearing the right clothes and owning the right gadgets.

Pam and I were not at all sure we wanted to expose our daughter to this. We were leaning heavily toward home-schooling (or boat-schooling, as the case may be) Breana and her future siblings. The idea of pulling up anchor and sailing away was calling to us with more and more urgency. We were starting to believe that traveling around the world, introducing the family to a smorgasbord of cultures, might be the only sane way to raise children with respect, open-mindedness, critical thinking, self-reliance, and a sense of true global citizenship. What had started as an escapist pipedream was slowly starting to seem like the most responsible choice we could make as parents.

Yet here was this perfect building, begging to be developed.

Trying to weigh these competing priorities was making us insane. On one hand buying the new building made amazing sense. On the other hand, how did we reconcile a gigantic urban real estate project, and the huge risk and commitment it would entail, with the yearning we were both feeling to pull up stakes, simplify our lives, and live by the values we wanted to teach our kids?

One evening Pam and I were talking after dinner, rehashing the pros and cons of the deal for the umpteenth time, when she said to me, "I heard this guy on the radio today, pitching some new self-help book. Sounded pretty dumb but he said one thing that caught my ear. He said that people get trapped by either/or thinking. As in, you have to be either a cat person or a dog person, either a liberal or a conservative. And these are totally artificial distinctions."

"Oka-a-ay," I said, waiting for more.

"Well, his point was that we do the same thing in our lives. We think we have to either make money or do what our heart desires; either marry a responsible partner or our romantic soul-mate. So we sell out important parts of our dreams without even realizing it."

"That's true, I guess." I still didn't know where she was headed.

"The trick, he said, is to use both/and thinking, like, 'I want to both make money and do what my heart desires.' Either/or thinking forces us to choose between things that are important to us; pitting one set of values against another. Both/and thinking frees our minds to come up with creative, breakthrough solutions that satisfy all our needs and values."

"So what are you saying, that we're being too either/or here?"

"Well, aren't we?" she asked. "What if we looked at it differently? What if we assumed we could have it all? Everything we want?"

No sooner had she framed this question than the answer to our dilemma became incredibly obvious. It was an answer that had been right under our nose the whole time and synthesized everything.

"Okay, we so buy the building at 123 West 15th Street and design the hell out of it. Really let our creative juices flow. Pull out all the stops."

"Build ourselves a great family space, one we'll absolutely love living in for several years."

"Pay off Jim Sandino."

"Pour all the values we believe in into our building design."

"Right. Create the coolest 'green' building we can come up with. Make it spectacular and enjoy the hell out of the ego gratification it gives us. Get some publicity. Create a buzz for the first green luxury condo complex in Manhattan."

"Let the kids do some growing up for a few years. Then…"

"Sell the condos for a hefty price tag. Pay off the banks, keep a nice little pile for ourselves."

"Then, when we're done having kids and they're all a little older, sail off into the sunset. Home-school them all."

"Yeah, boat-school them."

"Sail the seven seas, see the world, and live entirely on the rental income from our luxury, double-wide condo."

"Till we find a place, somewhere in the world, that we all fall in love with and decide to settle down again."

Both/and, not either/or.

We were in. Pam always knew how to get me.

CHAPTER SIX

WHAT HAVE WE GOTTEN OURSELVES INTO?

"*Conformity is the jailer of freedom and the enemy of growth*

John F. Kennedy

The purchase of 123 West 15th Street involved eight months of negotiations with the "eccentric" (a redundant term, perhaps, in Manhattan) owner Kathleen Brody, who had owned the building since 1996. She was piece of work right out of an old Woody Allen movie. A defiant, short, older woman that was a New Yorker true to the heart. It seemed that she just lived in the city too long and became reclusive and used her wrath to hide behind. The ironic part was that Mrs. Brody had actually bought the building one month after I'd bought mine next door in 1996. It had been done through a private sale. I would have bought it myself had I known at the time. Which only proves the thesis that you never really know what's going on next door in Manhattan until it's too late, and sometimes not even then.

We made a series of offers and counter-offers that led to endless stalling and nickel-and-diming tactics on the part of the seller. By this point in my life I had been through several closings and Mrs. Brody and her attorney were by far the most difficult people I'd ever dealt with. Some New Yorkers just live by their own rules and force everyone else to conform to their demands. It usually produces nothing of value, just delay and more costly delay. We'd run into the same thing when trying to buy out Jim Sandino. Brody knew we wanted the building and that we were the only game in town. So that gave her power. Power to stall, stymie, stonewall, and pump up the price.

Understandably, there might have been a little animosity between us. Why? Well, because we had sued her in June, 1998 to force her to repair the rear wall of her building. It had been pulling down the rear wall of our building at 121 West 15th Street due to neglect and disrepair. Her brick façade was five degrees off the vertical plane of the building and it adjoined ours. We were renovating our building at 121 West 15th and didn't want all our work to be in jeopardy because of her neglect. A city inspection confirmed our concerns and forced us to make her correct it for both of our sakes. But the insurance companies basically handled the cost—and her own building ended up better off for it—so we didn't think it should be a real problem between us.

Still, Brody insisted on making things difficult. She didn't want to provide any information on the building because (1) she didn't keep good records and (2) she wanted to be purposely vague so as to make the building look as attractive as possible. She refused to give us records on the tenants, and the rent roll history was sparse (a single page).

Brody's attorney, Joseph Leuzzi, had a long adversarial relationship with our closing attorney, Andy Albstein, which only added to the negotiation problems. There was no good faith basis to work from. Leuzzi spent most of his time trying to pull one over on us and school our attorney rather than do a straight negotiation. In order to minimize conflict, Andy was forced into a strategy of using junior partners to submit responses to Leuzzi and then personally responding to his comments in the rebuttal. Turns out this is common with legal egos in Manhattan, especially in real estate law where everyone knows each other. The combination of deliberate obfuscation and an attorney trying to skew the contract only added more time and delay.

The obtuseness of the sellers probably would have caused us to walk away unless we had already known the building by dint of living next door to it for the last ten years. We had friendly relationships with several of the tenants and they provided much of the missing information Mrs. Brody and our own eyes couldn't supply. So we were pretty well aware of what we were getting into and had been through the common areas of the building on several occasions.

James Nelson, our agent from Massey Knakal Real Estate, took us through all the rounds of bids and counter offers. We thought his tall blond WASP demeanor could get this deal done for us with Brody. She took a shine to him early on in negotiations and we hoped that would help in closing this deal. On August 12, 2003, Brody finally accepted our offer of $1,500,000. The catch was that we had to have a signed contract in ten days. Even in those days of quick closings, this turned out to be not enough time to get a bank commitment in writing to sign the contract. Unfortunately, Brody's counter offer was then accepted due to a negotiation blunder on the part of our broker, which added $100,000 to the final price. So we started out with additional expenses already.

The purchase of 123 West 15th Street closed four months later for $1,600,000 on October 22-23. It was a two-day closing, believe it or not, just because the seller wanted it that way. To pass time, Joseph Leuzzi showed us his antique used key collection. Something's you can't make up. A complete waste of our time.

The good news was, the purchase did solve the Sandino problem, as planned. One year after I purchased 123 West 15th Street, without yet having done anything substantial to improve the building, I was able to refinance it (via a pair of mortgages through Intervest Bank for $2,800,000 on 11/19/04) and pay off Mr. Sandino $719,033.45 towards his buyout. Then in January, 2005, I refinanced our first building, 121 West 15th Street, for $3,965,000 and was able to finish paying him off and take another $2,000,000 in cash to seed my development project to combine the two buildings.

The Sandinos were paid a total of $1,200,000 for their two-story condo for which they had put down $100,000 for in 1996. They moved out to Los Angeles and we never heard from them again. Jim still does some work in New York City and my documentary film crew (detailed in later chapters) chased him down for an interview. As you can imagine, he did not offer a very flattering perspective of me. After we settled the sale of the condo we had to withhold $40,000 for a built-in entertainment center that he ripped out of the wall and moved with him. He thought he could take built-ins with him after he sold them as part of the condo. Not too swift.

It is what it is.

Anyway, with the purchase complete, we could now begin our development project for real. Of course, long before the sale was complete, Pam and I had begun the planning and designing. Now the time had come to shake up our comfortable existence and push forward once more into the abyss.

Okay, so what had we bought ourselves?

We knew that the building was dilapidated and in dire need of a major gutting, like a lot of Single Room Occupancy buildings in Manhattan. So no surprise there. Mrs. Brody had undoubtedly added to her 46 outstanding safety violations by now, and we knew that too.

The building was a brownstone, technically registered with the Department of Housing as a "transient hotel." This was a holdover from the old Vaudeville days when all the playhouses were on 14th Street, and the performers and stagehands needed temporary rooms. As transient housing, we didn't even have a certificate of occupancy.

The building also had a dark history as a brothel where German spies conspired to blow up the Black Tom ammunition dump behind the Statue of Liberty in July, 1916. A lot of people may not realize that September 11, 2001 was not the first time New York City was openly attacked by U.S. enemies. The Black Tom ammunition episode is written extensively by Chad Millman in his book The Detonators. According to the book, the explosion was massive, "pelting the statue of Liberty with shrapnel, devastating much of lower Manhattan, and casting a fiery orange glow over New York City... people as far away as Maryland felt the ground shake." A Wikipedia article reports, "Windows broke as far as 25 miles away, including thousands in lower Manhattan. Some window panes in Times Square were completely shattered. The stained glass windows in St. Patrick's Church were destroyed." Had CNN existed at the time, we would have had our 9/11 panic nearly a century earlier.

The three German spies that masterminded the explosion later committed suicide in the basement of our newly purchased building at 123 West 15th Street, when the police surrounded the building back in 1916. We always thought the saboteurs would have enjoyed the fact that we were putting a garage in the basement, which would likely house German-made luxury cars.

History aside, 123 West 15th Street was a blight to the neighborhood. One of its more pleasant tourist features, for example, were the cups of urine that would appear daily on the second floor windowsills on the front of the building. This was due to the tenants' sheer laziness and refusal to walk to the bathroom down the hall at night. It was easier to take the closest plastic cup, fill 'er up, and place it on your window ledge. And it was the women who did this. Go figure. Of course, given the state of the bathrooms, I might have made the same choice.

The building hadn't had a super or even someone who cleaned the hallways and bathrooms once a week! It was disgusting to a degree that words can't capture.

The building needed a major boost to begin its second life. We were planning to give it one. Since we had already renovated 121 West 15th Street, we figured we had a leg up on the project. The two were sister buildings. They were both set up the same structurally and had been built together in 1853.

We soon discovered that 123 was in way worse shape than 121 had ever been. 123 had not had any real maintenance since the 1930s. There were patchwork repairs everywhere you looked—everything from newspapers stuffed in the walls for insulation to electrical wiring done with speaker wires. All the floors were sloped and were rotting through in several places. The plumbing was a combination of PVC piping and old cast iron pipes joined together with duct tape. The sink elbows in all the rooms leaked from years of tenants' using them as urinals—the uric acid had literally burned holes in the metal. The electrical system hadn't been upgraded since the 1930s and still used those ancient glass fuses that looked like shotgun shells. (I found one little lighting/hardware store in the Village where I could buy replacement fuses, and boy I was a regular customer.) If the nine tenants all turned on their AC units at the same time, several fuses would blow, so they kept a box of glass fuses by the electrical box. These were rated at 30 amps for a 15-amp circuit. Extremely dangerous, but that was the only way the circuit would work with the extra load. You could actually feel the wires getting warm when this happened. Basically the building was a death trap waiting to be tripped.

Mrs. Brody took pride in the fact that she'd done the absolute minimum of upkeep. It was her deliberate attempt to persuade the tenants to move out as soon as possible. Completely illegal, of course. But effective; she'd cut the population in half and succeeded in angering all those tenants that did remain.

The building had some interesting features as well. By doing a little research we learned that 121, 123, 125, and 127 West 15th Street had all been built at the same time. There were hidden doorways on the sidewalls on each floor. These doorways had at one time connected all four buildings together so the contractors could work on them at the same time. The idea was that workers could move wheelbarrows full of materials from one building to the next without going down to the street and back up. Once all the structural work was done and the doorways were no longer needed, the plasterers sealed them over. Those were the days of lath and plaster, no sheet rock. We'd found some of those old doorways when we renovated 121 West 15th Street.

What about the rental conditions?

Well, for those who don't know what SRO living is like, a good example can be seen in the movie Taxi Driver with Robert DeNiro. Deniro's character, Travis Bickle, lived in a SRO. A SRO is a room—typically quite small—in a building that rents out rooms, not apartments. Bickle's room was actually large by Manhattan standards. SROs often are no larger than eight by ten feet with a sink and a small refrigerator in them. The bathroom/shower and toilet are in separate rooms down the hall and shared by all the tenants on a floor. There is no cooking in the rooms unless they have a designated kitchen.

At 123 West 15th Street we had three larger units in addition to many eight-by-tens. These bigger ones were ten by twenty, with kitchens and private bathrooms, but the kitchens were rarely used. Takeout was king at 123 West15th Street, as was diabetes from the salt-rich diet. It is what it is.

Obviously, rent is low for these habitations. Because of the low rent, turnover is also low. The rent increases were voted on each year through the Rent Guidelines Board, which typically didn't allow more than a 2% bump per year at that time. The rents our tenants were paying ranged from $175.53 to $672.94 per month, depending on how long the tenant had lived there. The longer you live there, the lower the rent, because it only goes up 2% a year. (When and if a unit actually became vacant—and this was rare because residents often passed their units on to relatives—you could raise the rent a bit more. Turnover was really the only way to increase rent.) Keep in mind that rent included electricity, heat, and water. Owners are allowed to charge extra for tenants with air conditioning but even that is carefully regulated and works out to only a few extra dollars a month for the landlord. Very rarely does a regulated apartment stay empty unless the building is being renovated. Why do you think NY renters read the obituaries to find an apartment?

The Rent Guidelines Board controls all aspects of SROs and rent-stabilized buildings through a series of complicated, arcane regulations all in favor of the tenant. The tenants have the legal right to remain in their apartments until they wish to leave or they die—and even after their death their relatives can still retain legal rights to their apartments. Consequently, the tenants really have no incentive to keep their space maintained and cleaned. There is no penalty for failing to do so. The building owner cannot legally evict them.

It is simply not economical in many rent-controlled buildings to put money into maintaining the building, because, by law, you'll only receive a fraction of the expenses back in rent increases. In most cases the land and air space is worth more than the building. (Manhattan, being essentially a vertical town, is the only place where air rights are a substantial consideration.) In our case, the nine tenants we inherited were paying a combined rent of less than $4200 per month. That barely covered the utility bills and insurance for the building; forget about the mortgage or a repairs budget.

You might imagine that SROs are vitally needed in order to help house the army of low-paid workers that keep Manhattan ticking. That may be true to some extent, but for many people SRO living is a lifestyle choice, not a necessity. I personally know of several people who live in SROs and work at decent-paying jobs. They make the deliberate choice to live in a SRO because they're able to save a lot of money living this way. Then they take extensive overseas vacations with their savings. I can think of three tenants in a neighboring SRO at 119 West 15th Street who do just this. So not everyone is stuck in this situation. Some don't work for whatever reason and live on disability. Some choose SRO living in order to rebuild their lives, and some game the system to live a nicer lifestyle for a portion of the year.

Single Room Occupancies were set up in major cities in the U.S. after

World Wars I and II to get people back to work in the cities and build the economy up again. The idea was to provide inexpensive housing near where the employment was. These regulations were dissolved in most major cities in the Seventies and Eighties. Not in Manhattan, though. Originally, SROs were a good idea to jumpstart the work force, but their usefulness has since been eclipsed. Antiquated laws shift all the burden from the tenants to the landlords without offering any real incentive for the landlords. Which is why you end up with falling-down deathtraps like 123 West 15th Street was when we bought it.

There are roughly a million rent-regulated apartments in Manhattan today. That's way down from the huge number in the Fifties, but they still create an artificial market. And it's a market that's subsidized by the building owners rather than the government. The laws seriously restrict the rights of property owners and limit what they can do with their own property. At the same time, the artificially low rents allow tenants to live beyond their means and not seek better-paying work. The system is non-evolutionary.

The other main problem with rent regulation is the archaic manner in which the Rent Guidelines Board calculates increases in operating expenses for owners. The Rent Regulation Board typically allows only a minimal rent increase of 1 to 2% a year, while new regulations and real-world inflation raise operating expenses by 9 to 15 percent a year. Again, the burden is borne by the landlord while the tenant is artificially insulated from the realities of the economy.

The first thing you have to do when you buy a rent-stabilized building is join the RSA (Rent Stabilization Association). The RSA facilitates the owners' keeping up with all the regulations required for rent-stabilized buildings. And there are tons of them. Every year you have to provide the rent rolls of your building. Any changes to the building must be documented and signed off by each tenant, from smoke detectors and carbon monoxide indicators to mailbox changes. Documentation is the rule of the day.

All that is just to own the building. (The tenants, in effect, own their SRO apartments, not you.) Renovating a rent-stabilized building; now that's a joy-fest of an entirely different magnitude. The rules and regulations are complex enough to make federal tax law look like the rulebook to Candy land. Knowing this, we sought out the best attorneys we could find, before we even bought the building, and were introduced to Belkin Burden Wenig & Goldman LLP. Joe Burden is one of the best housing regulation attorneys in the city. We needed a good understanding of what legal steps needed to be taken to renovate a SRO building, along with likely time frames these actions would take.

Based on Joe Burden's advice, the initial plan, as I mentioned, was to renovate two floors for our accommodations while leaving the other floors as SROs and let them empty out through attrition. Because we purchased 123 West 15th Street in our own names, not as a corporation, regulations allowed us to convert it into a home for our family relatively quickly. All we needed in order to commence work was a Certificate of No Harassment.

A Certificate of No Harassment states that the owner has not done anything in the last two years that can be considered harassment of the current and past tenants. It must be attested to by all the tenants and is strictly required before any renovations can be made. You not only have to get all of the current residents to sign, you have to track down previous tenants and post it in the paper that you are petitioning the court to get this certificate. Which helps explain why there hadn't been any major renovating done by the previous owner. No way could Mrs. Brody have gotten a thumbs-up from her whole tenant roster.

I thought we'd have a relative walk in the park, though. First of all, we were new owners, so what could we have done to harass the tenants or build up bad blood? The tenants all knew us; we'd been neighbors for the last ten years. We had good relationships with most of them and they seemed to be looking forward to a more responsive landlord. That's why I had made a point, right off the bat, to meet with each tenant individually and take care of any problems they had with the building. I'd immediately started making basic repairs in areas like plumbing and electrical, and had initiated a weekly cleaning.

So getting a Certificate of No Harassment should have been the least of my worries, right?

Ah, my innocent child, you still have much to learn of the Ways of Gotham.

CHAPTER SEVEN

MEET THE TENANTS

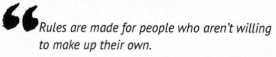

Rules are made for people who aren't willing to make up their own.

Chuck Yeager

Even though the tenants seemed to generally like us, getting access to their rooms was a different matter entirely. Many of them had had so little contact with their previous landlord(s), and were so accustomed to living insulated lives, that they really thought of their rooms as their own private kingdom. The pro-tenant slant of the housing regulations further encouraged this kind of thinking. Anyway, a lot of the tenants would not even let me in their rooms. Pretty hard to make assessments when you can't cross the threshold.

Once we finally got in, I could see why they kept us out. Not only was there an incredible amount of filth and damage—ruined window frames, urine smells, holes in walls and floors, feces, insect colonies, unsanitary hoarding—but many of the rooms also had evidence of illegal cooking and self-designed wiring systems that were begging to start a fire. Some of the rooms had obviously been illegally sub-let as well; the tenants were renting them out for profit. Hardly just a New York thing, of course.

The first thing we had to do was to get everybody signed on a lease. Since the previous owner did not have correct leases and since legally the building was a transient hotel, many tenants did not have leases at all. So we sent out six-month leases in 2004 on the anniversary of their move-in dates, which would have to be renewed every six months. The point was to make sure our rent rolls were registered with the Rent Stabilization Authority and that the tenants were on record as accepting of their rents. That took one problem out of the equation. The tenants were now legally entered into the system should an eviction process ever be required for any of them.

When you buy a rent-regulated building such as a SRO, you have to come into it with the right mindset or it will drive you insane. You need to really get the fact that while you have all the obligations of owning the building—if someone slips on the sidewalk out front, you will get sued—you have few of the benefits. Because I'd met with attorney Joe Burden I knew what I was walking into and had a pretty good understanding of the process involved in dealing with tenants and getting them to eventually vacate the premises.

In truth, I had no real argument with the lengthy process. I understood where tenants were coming from and actually supported the spirit of the regulations. I knew these rooms were their homes and I wanted to be totally respectful of that. I think you need to put yourself in the tenants' shoes; otherwise you get into an "us versus them" mentality and I didn't want that to happen. I knew many of the tenants personally and even considered a couple of them friends. I didn't want to screw them or ruin their lives or kick them out on the streets. I just wanted to work out a mutually satisfactory long-term plan.

Of course, when you're in Manhattan, institutional insanity gets in the way. The Certificate of No Harassment (CNH) is a great example. Without this certificate you can be fined for renovating your own building. The CNH basically states that the landlord has not done anything negative to the tenant to unduly influence him to vacate his apartment. Though the purpose of the law is to prevent landlords from booting tenants out of their rooms indiscriminately, what it boils down to, in practice, is a disincentive to make any improvements to your building. See, if you have even one tenant with an axe to grind against you, that tenant can refuse to sign the CNH, which prevents you from making upgrades to the building that would benefit everyone.

So most landlords don't bother.

The more immediate problem with the CNH, though, is that tenants are not idiots. Many of them know that if you are asking them to sign a CNH, you're up to something. Change be comin'. They see the writing on the wall and they know their time as tenants may be running out. They also know they're holding a card you need, and they smell money. I understand the position they're in. That's how the rules have been set up. Really, what does a tenant have to lose? If your life is going to be seriously disrupted, why not try to get something out of the deal? What's more American than that?

I had anticipated this kind of thing and had actually budgeted for it with a "buyout" fund for tenants. But, as with everything else in Manhattan real estate, Murphy's Laws kick in, specifically the two that state, "Anything that can go wrong will go wrong," and "Everything takes longer than you think." (There should be another one: "Everything costs more than you think it will.") It ended up taking six months of negotiations with tenants and their attorneys before we could obtain the CNH we needed to start renovating the building. That was only the beginning. The initial renovation plan fell through because the structure of the building was in such bad shape that it would not allow us to start renovating from the ground and work our way up. Eventually it took another two years of negotiations to finally empty the building. And the costs to us? Holy crap. With a few of the tenants we went through straight negotiations, no lawyers; a couple of them went all the way to court; and four of them ended up in long, drawn-out suits that went on for years.

Here is a little snapshot of the tenants—the eclectic mix of doormen, construction workers, city employees, and general oddballs you find in rooming houses all over the city—and the eventual outcomes of their tenancies.

Dru Lockwood, Rent $500. Dru was a tall, skinny guy who lived on top floor. Never knew him too well. Just an honest, decent guy who wanted to get his life restarted. He didn't like his original unit and agreed to move to an upper-floor unit for a preferred rent of $100 a month and to leave at end of the lease term on July 31, 2004. He left as promised and was no problem at all.

Norman Weisberg. I don't really count Norman as a tenant. He lived on the top floor, moved out of his own accord two months after I bought the building.

Ronald Hill, Rent $642.77. Another easy one. Ronald wrote a letter on February 4, 2004, stating that his room was substandard, and moved out three or four weeks later. He wanted to leave, even gave up his damage deposit without a fight because he broke his lease. He basically ran from the place as quickly as he could.

Hey, this was going pretty smoothly, right? Well...

Al Simon, Rent $289.25. Al was a bona fide character. A female wrestling promoter and small-time pimp. He'd run away from home at the age of 15 and had been living at 123 West 15th Street ever since. Al had been a friend of my family since we moved to the neighborhood in 1996 and Pam always had a birthday party for him, cooking him a nice dinner and baking him a cake. He always got great toys for the kids, little plastic things, not expensive, but fun for the kids. Big heart. He had a pleasant air about him and always wore a fun colorful hat over his jet black hair. Friendly to everyone and continuously striking up conservations with people on the street. The problem was you had to break off the discussion, because Al was in no rush to go anywhere, so he could talk to you all day.

Al became a severe diabetic by living off the McDonalds menu for decades on end. I think his sodium consumption (not to mention his sugar intake) was about 1497% of the Recommended Daily Allowance. His room was jammed full of car and train models and little working waterfalls (I counted 23 of them; one was four feet tall). Al was insane for trains; he collected books and videos on trains too. He had no space leftover for a bed so he slept in a reclining chair. The walls were decorated with multiple Christmas lights that ran from thirteen extension cords. He also had thirteen hanging, three-tier metal fruit baskets that held all of his possessions, including syringes for giving himself insulin shots. It was amazing what he crammed into that tiny space. NASA should have consulted with him.

Al "sold" his apartment to me for $52,500, no lawyers involved, and was given $20,000 of it to move upstairs to a smaller vacant room until the upper floors were demolished. We agreed he'd get the remainder when he vacated the building. But here's the funny thing: he didn't want to be paid in cash, but in electric trains. Yup. Al didn't have a credit card so, over time, he gave me $10,000 worth of orders for model trains, model buildings, and miniature set pieces, which I purchased for him and had shipped to a guy in New Jersey who was building a custom track layout for him. That's where the other ten grand went; to the track builder. The track was going to be 8 x 8 for his 8 x 10 room. Al was designing it to be built on a raised platform so he could put a bed and living quarters under it and have a spare two-foot area where he could stand and play with his trains. I wondered how quickly that setup would get old. All in all, I did about fifty purchases for him from every model train boutique in the U.S.

I physically helped him move out in '06 and stored his stuff for him until he got re-settled. He later had to have a few toes amputated and was put into an elderly home in Chinatown. We kept in touch with him for a while. Pam and I used to visit him and bring him Pam's brownies, but eventually he slipped off the radar and we lost contact with him.

I ended up storing his stuff for four years for free and eventually brought it to his place in Chinatown. Al never got to see his train set finished; the track guy kept everything.

Richard Joyce, Rent $278.55. Another long-timer. Richard was a taxi driver who did Tae Kwon Do on the roof in his shorts every day and constantly read pulp fiction. He was over 6" 5', skinny as a rail. Drove a cab every night, late shift, and slept during the day. He must have had a few stories he could have sold to Taxicab Confessions. Had a punching bag in his room, bunk beds, and a hanging chair made of bamboo. That was it. On the sink was ten years' worth of change in a pile. When he moved out I cashed it in for him (this was before there were change machines in banks) and he ended up with over $500. His deal was a straight negotiation, sans lawyers; final tally $48,000.

John Gallagher, Rent $564.13. John was an actor. You may have spotted him in The Darjeeling Express, Meet the Parents, Extremely Loud and Incredibly Close, and other movies and TV shows like Boardwalk Empire. John had moved into his room, one of our largest ones, in the 1980s in the middle of a ten-year drinking binge. Told me he lost an entire decade to booze. He worked as a real estate agent in the city, mostly doing rentals to college kids for first apartments. He started to get serious about acting in the '90s and it kept him away from the bottle. He took acting classes with some famous NY people, including Susan Sarandon who lived on our block when she was with Tim Robbins. When I met with John after buying the building, he complained that he couldn't bring women home to his place so he negotiated an exit deal with me over several meetings at a Chinese restaurant on 6th Avenue. Our original agreement netted him $15,000 upon signing and $75,000 upon vacating, but he ended up trying to stick me for another $20,000. He eventually backed off on that and we paid him $90,000 total.

Peter Kelly, Rent $165.18. Peter was the doorman at the Vanmeer (on 7th Ave., between 15th & 14th Street). He was divorced when he moved into the SRO, took the cheapo quarters so he could put his son through dental school and pay alimony. Pete was a nice Irish guy with a classic red nose. No thwarter of stereotypes, he went through about two cases of beer a week. I would help him carry it up every Sunday. Sweet guy and very stand-up. His stance on moving out was, "Gimme ten grand that I can give my son and I'll go live in his pool house and play with my grandkids for the rest of my life." The day came for him to leave, I handed the family the check, they took his clothes in trash bags, and he was gone.

Michael Harrison, Rent $590.67. Not a sweet guy. Hostile construction worker, pissed off at the world, never a smile. Refused to talk to me (for what reason, I don't know), slipped notes under my door. Called in complaints on me all the time. Unstable as hell. He lived next to Al and used to pound on Al's door because he was sure Al was interfering with his cell phone reception. Same thing with his cable (the fact that cable is hard-wired didn't faze him). Just for kicks, Harrison would call the city's 311 number at four in the morning to complain that there was no hot water. He did this about once a week during the winter. The city would send someone out to bang on my door at five a.m. and we'd both have to go check the water with a thermometer. It was always hot, but not too hot, perfectly within legal limits. This was one of our earliest examples of people using the 311 complaint system for personal vendettas. Eventually the city would just call me and I'd tell them the water temperature by phone and that was that. Harrison and Meyer were the only two who fought me on the CNH. Harrison was the second last tenant to leave. We gave him free rent from January 2005 through October, 2006, and a total payout of $30,000.

Eugene Cory, Rent $414.57. Mr. Cory was a left wing activist and copywriter who wrote a political newsletter. Well, "active" might be the wrong root word to use for Mr. Cory. Very corpulent dude, long gray hair, unshaven. Had a couple cats living with him and no litter box. You couldn't talk to him through the door for more than a minute without being bowled over by the ammonia smell. Cory had been in his room for over twenty years, but it smelled like his cats had been there since the Big Bang. He was a major pain to extract. Got himself a ponytail-and-black-turtleneck attorney who took a big chunk of his settlement in the end. The guy put me through six hours of depositions, grilling me on who I was, what I did, where I came from, and what I was doing at 123 West 15th Street. It was a pure fishing expedition to find anything they could use to wangle a higher payout.

Cory hired movers to move him out and it took over two days— for a twin 8 x 10 room! Lucky me, he ended up moving into 119 West 15th Street, on the other side of my home at 121. I'm sure a lot of the complaints that came in on my building were from him. I actually felt bad for the guy. The $58,000 we paid him was all gone within a year and he was eventually evicted from his new digs.

Robert Meyer, Rent $601.52. Ah, Robert, Robert, Robert. Squirrely guy in his fifties, around five-three, brown hair, kept to himself. Worked the night shift as a janitor in some school in Harlem and wrote screenplays during the day. I don't think he showed them to anybody. Meyer was a crafty one. I guess all that movie plotting paid off because he played us as if we were the warden in The Shawshank Redemption. He knew that the last person to negotiate out of the building would have the most leverage, so he just bided his time. We signed a contract with him in exchange for the CNH, which spelled out that he could live there until 2010. We wanted him to leave much sooner than that, and thought the construction in the building would eventually become so annoying he would feel compelled to vacate. We even added a clause that if he left prior to the move-out date he would get an additional $40,000. But he held out and held out, knowing, I guess, that his leverage would only increase as time went on.

He had moved from a room on the first floor with kitchen and private bathroom to a room that was 8 by 10 feet, with the bathroom and shower down the hall on the top floor. He was the last tenant left and he stayed on till the building was reduced to a shell, with only a staircase to the third floor and his room and a bathroom remaining; all the other rooms gutted to brick and frame walls. No sane person would live like that, we reasoned. Nor would a sane person put up with active demolition going on around him five days a week. But Meyer knew all he had to do was wait us out. Last man standing wins. He was right. We finally pried him out with a crowbar at the end of August, 2006, to the tune of $250,000. Yep, that's right. A quarter million. To leave our building. In much of America you can buy a building for that amount.

There were also a few tenants who moved in on a temporary basis after we bought the building. One of these tenants ended up costing us some money, too.

Sophie Rogers-Gessert, Rent $1850.00. She rented a strung-together combo of three SROs as an apartment. She signed a two-year lease in July of 2005, with the stipulation that she would have to vacate the building when we gave her a six-month notification of the gutting of the building. Completely legal and fully executed. This was one of our first experiences of legal contracts not being treated as binding, but used as a business tool for negotiation. We exercised our six-month notice in March of 2006. She was okay with it verbally, but then hired an attorney, Alan Goldberg, who decided to make trouble. He cited us for insufficient hot water, defective electricity, lack of an individual mailbox, unsafe construction, and rodent infestation. Sophie then spent the next month calling 311 on us for anything she could make up. I had the inspectors on speed dial at that point. None of the accusations were proven, but in our legal system it doesn't matter. We went to court. She is in the article in the Times about us and the documentary video (both of which I'll get to shortly). She knew she was in the wrong but smelled money.

We tried to settle before trial, but no luck. On the first day of court the judge asked the parties to negotiate something and not waste the court's time. They wanted $100,000, we were offering $30,000, and we settled at $60,000. She thought she'd won the lottery, but became quite the unhappy camper when her lawyer took his big bite. C'est la vie. (That's French for "It is what it is.")

Even though we'd known it would not be painless, quick, or easy to render our building tenant-free, we had no idea what kind of time and energy it would consume. Between the meetings, negotiations, court appearances, letters, and phone calls, the emptying of 123 became a major part of our lives for the better part of two years (continuing, at a lesser level, for months and years to come).

This was a major reality check for Pam and me. We had been by no means naïve going into this thing, but I think in the back of our minds we still believed that if you were respectful and treated people as you would want to be treated, things would work out for everyone. We had no interest in "screwing over" any of our tenants. We knew we were causing a major disruption to their lives, so we wanted to be as liberal as possible with our exit timelines and financial arrangements. In most parts of the country it would probably seem absurd to even think of buying your own property back from renters, but this was Manhattan. So we were prepared to pay. We thought we were being as humane and accommodating as could possibly be expected. We knew there'd be some hiccups but we had no idea how much money and energy this would set us back. All before we did a speck of renovation. I can only imagine how much worse it would have been if we had taken a neglectful or adversarial approach.

All told, it cost us roughly $525,000 in tenant costs, plus an attorney fee of over $350,000—so, pretty damn close to a million dollars—and three years of time to vacate our building so that we could even start construction on the project. More than once we asked ourselves why we weren't just renting. It certainly would have made our lives a lot simpler.

And maybe we could have sued someone and ended up in the black a lot sooner. But we didn't want to go to the dark side. At least not yet.

DESiGN AND CONQUER

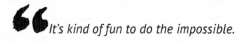*It's kind of fun to do the impossible.*

Walt Disney

We gave our 123 West 15th Street building project a name, Valhalla, which
we thought would be fitting. In Norse mythology, Valhalla was a majestic,
opulent hall of mythical proportions where heroes dwelled. (121 West 15th
Street project was to be named Fólkvangr, Valhalla's Sister Hall.) The name
sort of captured the grand vision we had for our development. Unfortunately,
Norse Valhalla was a place you reached only after dying in battle. We had no
idea how fitting the name would turn out to be in the end.

There were several major steps to getting the Valhalla project rolling: moving
out the old tenants, doing the design work and getting it approved, finding
the contractors to do all of the highly specialized work, and, of course, getting
the construction financing in place. As all this was going on, Pam and I had
very full dance cards in other areas of our lives. I was managing Better Lists
Inc., a direct mail fulfillment company with thirteen employees, working 60-
plus hours a week while doing a reverse commute to Stamford, Connecticut
daily. Because it was my business, I could juggle my schedule as needed
while dedicating another 60 hours a week to the building project. Pam, a
former fashion model (one of the original Jordache Girls, with a twelve-year
modeling career), worked full-time, too, doing product development for
Maidenform, commuting to New Jersey. She also ran Terrapin Chelsea Art
Gallery LLC, an online art gallery that held openings for the artists at our
home once a month. We had just gotten our Sailboat Googolplex, an X-412
racing sailboat, delivered in May, 2003, and I had a full summer campaign of
six regattas lined up, which I would be racing with my crew of twelve. Pam

and I traveled extensively, also, spending Christmas in Cortina, Italy. Insane? Maybe, but we both had a ton of energy in those days. We worked hard and played hard. We also had a great live-in au pair from Denmark who helped us out with Breana.

The numerous developmental steps of the Valhalla project, of course, were going on simultaneously, or at least overlapping one another. As we were moving the tenants out, we were also putting together the design and construction team, working on the financing, etc. It's cleaner to talk about each step separately, though, so I'll continue to do it that way.

The next major step was planning and design.

We had an overall vision for the project that featured several key ideas. First of all, we wanted to join the two buildings. That was a definite. (There were a lot of reasons for this. We wanted to have our "double-wide"-concept condo and back yard, to live in and later to rent out for income. We also wanted to put in an off-street parking facility, which you could only do if you had forty feet of sidewalk frontage. So we needed the two combined buildings to give us that.) Second, we wanted to use as much green technology as possible. In fact we wanted to lead the way on the eco-front and build the first truly green condo complex in Manhattan (not only to reflect our personal values, but also to garner publicity and add appeal for the upscale market). Third, we wanted our condos to be top-end, luxury living spaces that would sell for advanced seven-figure price tags. Finally, we wanted the building to make a statement creatively. We wanted to build something that would take your breath away. Otherwise, why bother? Life's too short.

Before we even got started on design, we got a lot of legal advice, as well as advice on housing regulations, architecture, construction, and engineering. We talked to experts who knew about the Department of Buildings and the Department of Transportation and all the other agencies we'd need approvals from. We didn't want any (bad) surprises.

The design and planning team we put together consisted of Alexander "Sasha" Gendell (young unproven talented architect), Andy Pisani (master of the DOB trenches, expeditor), Norfast Engineering (extremely knowledgeable mechanical and electrical engineers), Gilsanz Murray Steficek (highly recommended structural engineers), Corcoran Sunshine Marketing Group (top marketing, selling, and design consultation for real estate in the city), and Top Penthouse (first in the field of modular construction in Manhattan). And, of course Pam and myself (all in over our heads) as designers and developers.

The reason we brought the Corcoran Sunshine Marketing Group aboard early was that they were the best in the business at marketing and selling small developments in Manhattan. They had an outstanding reputation. We wanted to pick their brains on what amenities to design into the condos and to get a feel for what the potential market was looking for. Ours was a radical new design for Manhattan, never done before. It was going to use geothermal wells for heating, for example, and there were only eight of them in all of Manhattan at the time, two of which were at the Center for Architecture at LaGuardia Place. The Corcoran group loved our building concept and loved the idea of a boutique development done by a husband and wife team. They gave us some great advice during the planning stage.

Working with them and our architect, and using our most ambitious creative ideas, we came up with our design. A picture is worth a thousand words, so here is what it looked like:

If you prefer the thousand-word approach, here is how Corcoran advertised it:

> Quietly sited mid-block at the lush intersection of Chelsea and Greenwich Village, where east yields to west, 123 West 15th Street offers a limited collection of residences representing an avant–garde take on postmodern/expressionist design. A contextually-appropriate façade of brick masonry eases just three special owners home to expansive room dimensions where surfaces are active and right-angles are few. Indeed, drawing on multiple inspirations—aeronautical, geological, planetary—playfulness with arcilinearity (sic) is the hallmark of 123. In a nod to New Orleanian Franco-Spanish architecture, whirling ironwork adorns each home's private and extensive outdoor space. Additionally, the integration of green technologies, including, but not limited to, natural gas power generation and geothermic climate control, makes 123 a very special place to call home.

The eight-story building was going to consist of four condos: one triplex, two duplexes, one simplex, and three garage spaces. We would live in the Lower Duplex, which included the basement floor and first floor and was the only unit connected with 121 West 15th Street. The second floor would be a simplex (1027 square feet, front and back balconies, two wood-burning fireplaces, full bath, one bedroom). The third and fourth floor would be combined as the Middle Duplex (2054 square feet, front and back balconies on both floors, three fireplaces, two and a half baths, two bedrooms), and the fifth, sixth and seventh floor, along with the roof-deck floor, would make up the Penthouse Triplex (3220 square feet, front and back balconies on all floors, including roof deck, six fireplaces, four full bathrooms, three bedrooms). The Penthouse contained the most original design element: a cantilevered top section that doubled back over the building at 121 West 15th to make creative use of the air space over the (soon to be) lower of the two buildings. The triplex had unobstructed views of the Empire State building off the rear and the new World Trade Center in the front.

As for other design features and amenities, you could fill a book with them (and we did). Here are just a few of the high points:

- Large, curved, street-facing balconies, each accessed by a floor-to-ceiling NanaWall folding door system www.nanawallsystems.com with new Orleans style cast iron railings on front and back

- Ductless air conditioning from geothermal energy cooling

- Radiant colored cement floor for heating and cooling from geothermal energy throughout all condos and decks

- Custom monorail track lighting

- Bushed steel custom elevator with bamboo interior and locking buttons for each condo's access

- Natural green roof

- Natural gas emergency generator that could power both buildings and elevator in a black out

- Color video intercom at three entrance locations to the building and multiple locations in each condo

- Electric radiant heated custom curved brick sidewalk for deicing (no snow shoveling needed)

- Outdoor gas grills for each condo hooked up to gas line (no propane)

- DGA security card entry system (no keys)

- Private garage with car lift and car turntable, with remote control
  for three cars

- Asymmetric three-story solarium designed as a sail curved backward

- Top floor view of Empire State Building and World Trade Center

- Full roof deck with ivy modulation cover screen

- Trex wood teak deck www.Trex.com, with luxury portable gas grill hooked up to exterior gas line.

- Built-in speakers throughout the interior and exterior decks hooked to the entertainment center for each condo.

- Custom exterior wall glass light slits that fracture light (we designed these)

- Hidden light switches triggered by hand motion

- Custom chandeliers (in penthouse) that appear as floating pieces of paper by Gray Design

- Top-of-line appliances, cement counters, bamboo-finished cabinets

- Undulating wave ceiling design (vs. boxing in the beams)

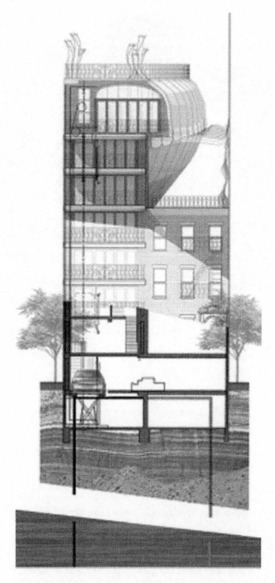

• Two geothermal wells (950 feet and 650 feet in depth) for heating and cooling

• Custom inverted two-sided fireplaces with gas and chimney fans

•   Top-of-line fixtures for all bathrooms, Jacuzzi tubs

An important aspect of the design was that there would be a ten-foot setback at the 60-foot level and the building would then go up to 75 feet. Keep in mind that with a ten-foot setback anything above 60 feet would not be visible from the street, physically impossible to see. Practically speaking, you would only see the front five stories of the building; it would be impossible to see the solarium or top floors from ground level. This was a major premise of our design and would become important later.

A particularly exciting aspect of the design and construction was that the top three floors would be designed modularly. This work was to be done by Top Penthouse, the only company in Manhattan doing modular construction at the time. I'd found them at a construction trade show. Modular construction was being widely done in Europe, especially in London, but it was a new concept in NYC. The idea was that each floor would consist of four to five modular sections, which would be built off-site with all the electrical, mechanical, plumbing, and interior work pre-installed. The premade sections would then be hoisted onto the building, linked together, and finished out in six to eight weeks. Done. The best part was that most of the construction would be done in a warehouse in New Jersey that wasn't affected by weather or by permissible work hours in the city. The teams could work around the clock. This was a lot more efficient way to build, especially in a city of eight million, and we thought this aspect alone would get our project some attention (and save us some money).

The trick was that the maximum size of each modular unit needed to be limited to the size of a fifty-foot semi-trailer. Anything bigger would require special arrangements to get into Manhattan. It would have to go over the George Washington Bridge, late at night only, very expensive. The plan was to have the floors arrive in stages. Each day one unit would show up, get unloaded, craned up to the top of the building, and attached to the other units. The following week the next floor would arrive the same way, one section at a time. Then it was just finish work: pouring the floor connections, attaching all the mechanical, electrical, and plumbing leads to other leads built into the top of the building.

Pam and I were bursting with excitement over this extremely ambitious and groundbreaking design. It was everything we'd hoped for and more.

We hoped the rest of the world would share our vision...

CHAPTER NINE

DESIGN APPROVAL BEGINS

> ❝ *The struggle is always between the individual and his sacred right to express himself and the power structure that seeks conformity, suppression, and obedience.*
>
> William O. Douglas

We believed in our Valhalla concept and had assembled a team of people who felt the same way. Now it was time to see if the world agreed. To begin with, we needed to have our plans approved by the DOB (Department of Buildings). We anticipated that this would be a fairly complex process, which might involve several rounds of back-and-forth with the DOB as issues came up and revised plans were submitted. We certainly didn't entertain any fantasies that after our first submission some cigar-smoking bureaucrat would stamp APPROVED in big red letters across our plans—full steam ahead. On the other hand, we did expect it to be a finite process, one with a beginning and end, and that once our plans were approved we could confidently proceed with construction.

We did not realize that plans could be reviewed, re-reviewed, re-re-reviewed, re-re-re-reviewed, re-re-re-re-reviewed, and arbitrarily changed on a constant and ongoing basis, with no regard for the costs and setbacks to the builder, or that any nut-job with a vested interest in obstructing our development could get the ear of DOB and make our lives miserable.

Yet another lesson to learn. It is what it is.

Now, a normal person—i.e. someone outside the construction industry— might assume that the Department of Buildings in a huge, modern city that's widely regarded as the economic and cultural center of America, if not the entire world, would be a well-structured, highly organized office that would oversee the rules of construction and zoning in an even, fair, and consistent manner. After all, Manhattan is known for some of the largest skyscrapers in the world and for some of the most complex and challenging building projects ever attempted by man. And all of this needs to be managed on a busy, densely populated 23-square-mile island that sees an influx of two-and-a-half million commuters a day. So New York's DOB must have state-of-the-art systems for enforcing its building codes and streamlined procedures for adhering to them. Right? Because if it didn't, that would be just plain silly.

Sigh.

What you also have to realize is that Manhattan is a very old city that still has building laws on its books from the 1700s and thrives on bureaucracy. Like Boston, which evolved organically from a network of random cow paths, Manhattan construction contains ideas, systems, protocols, and even equipment that goes back to the days of horses and buggies. Believe it or not, there are still wooden pipes in the water works of the city. So what you have is a complicated layer of old-world laws trying to shake hands with new-world construction and building techniques. And not trying particularly hard. Why not? Well, because the people who work in these offices have no personal interest in moving your project forward efficiently and nothing whatsoever to lose if it doesn't. In fact, just the opposite. Many of these people might stand to lose their jobs if the system were ever streamlined and modernized.

I think of government bureaucracy as something like a Galapagos Tortoise. Have you ever wondered why the Galapagos Tortoise is so huge, sluggish, and lumbering? One simple reason. Because it has no natural enemies. Nothing hunts the Galapagos Tortoise or competes with it for food; there's nothing to keep it sharp or to encourage it to evolve speed or competitive instincts. So it just keeps growing bigger and slower by the evolutionary century. It has no incentive to change. So it is with government bureaucracy. There is no free-market competition to keep it honest or accountable. It's the only game in town, so it doesn't need to be efficient or customer-friendly. After all, where are you going to go if you don't like the service—Jiffy Lube? Like the Galapagos Tortoise, government bureaucracy just keeps growing bigger, slower, lazier, less responsive, and more oblivious.

Welcome to the DOB in New York.

The first thing you have to realize, as I mentioned earlier, is that it takes about six or eight weeks just to get an appointment to sit down with a DOB official. After the initial rounds of communications, which typically take a couple of weeks, you have to request a meeting. It then takes a few weeks for them to respond to your request, and then they give you a meeting date a few weeks out from that. (Meanwhile your building site might be shut down for a relatively minor violation and you might be paying contractors to sit around doing nothing.)

The first time I entered the DOB offices, I had to rub my eyes to make sure I wasn't hallucinating. I could barely see the inspector, because his desk was walled off on three sides by stacked boxes filled with paper copies of building plans. Yes, paper. Everything is still done on hard copy at the DOB, not computers. There are boxes of papers stacked everywhere and you have to rely on the memory of the inspector to recall which box contains which document.

Needless to say, the inspectors at DOB can never find anything. One of the first things you learn about doing business with them is to bring duplicates of any paperwork you need to discuss, including documents they've already signed off on. Because if the DOB dude has to look for a document in his "files," while you're sitting with him, and you only have an hour, there goes your whole meeting time. And if you think the inspectors are disorganized you should see the office of the deputy commissioner, Max Lee. Jeez. I will never understand that management style. He would make Ignatius J. Reilly from the Confederacy of Dunces look organized.

Not only are the DOB's rules and laws misleading, arcane, and contradictory with one another, but there is deep corruption and graft engrained in the department. It's so bad that every seven years or so all the building inspectors are usually fired and replaced or moved on to new jobs. The reason? To disrupt the stream of payola. Most of the stories you read about major construction accidents in New York end up tracing back to some payoff of an inspector who didn't do his inspection correctly. This killer combination of autocracy, corruption, and the Galapagos Principle necessitates the hiring of an expeditor to get anything done.

An expeditor works for you. For a fee, he basically pushes your job through so that your permit is issued quickly and correctly from the DOB or DOT (Department of Transportation). He has a working relationship with the inspectors at the DOB/DOT and knows how to get things through the system. Why the DOT too? Well, in NYC all sidewalk demolition and construction on or under sidewalks is under the domain of the Department of Transportation. If you want to do anything that involves a sidewalk, you need to get permits from DOT. This includes any plumbing and electrical hook-up with the city; it all goes under the sidewalk.

We had a great expeditor, Andy Pisani, who had helped us on our gut renovation of 121 West 15th Street. Andy had decades of experience working projects through the DOB. He was a godsend and a necessity. But dealing with Andy was a job in itself. He wasn't a huge fan of returning phone calls, so if I wanted him to do some things for me, I would need to show up outside his office, stupidly early in the morning, and hand him a to-do list in person before the work day began. I'd need to come armed with cashier's checks (which meant a special trip to the bank during bankers' hours the day before) because anytime you used a personal check, that would delay things another ten days.

Well, before we purchased the building in April 2003, we had Andy do a full review of the renovation possibilities for combining 123 West 15th Street with our building at 121. Since our new development was to be a unique green design, Andy advised us to get the complete project approved up front by DOB, rather than doing a self-approval—which, oddly enough, is permissible in Manhattan. That way, when we started the actual building process there would be fewer problems because the project was already approved by the city.

In those days—remember, the real estate boom was in full swing—developments were popping up all over the city and many developers had gotten into the habit of starting construction with only partially-approved plans. Essentially they would do a self-approval of their plans, then, as they built, they would do things like add on extra floors that weren't in the original plans and use air space they weren't approved to use. Once the project was completed, the DOB would do a review for the Certificate of Occupancy and would find out that the developers had overbuilt. But by then the damage was already done.

You know how in personal property cases they say, "Possession is nine-tenths of the law"? Well, in the world of building approvals, "Existence is nine-tenths of the law." Once a building or an addition actually exists (i.e. someone has built it, legally or illegally), the DOB is reticent to make it stop existing. Only on rare occurrences did the government ever force these illegal expansions to be removed. The way it usually worked was that the condo units were sold quickly (often before construction was even complete) and by the time the DOB got off its ass to take action, a third party usually owned the property and then the whole thing would be delayed in court. Et cetera, et cetera. You get the picture. But by the time we started our project the DOB was beginning to be proactive and rein in on self-approvals and they were no longer allowed.

We didn't want to take that risk anyway. We knew our project would bring a lot of attention to it. We wanted to remove all potential problems and nail down all needed approvals well before our development became public knowledge. After all, there were a lot of possible stumbling blocks in our design—a driveway, a car lift to a subterranean garage with a turntable, oversized balconies on the front and back of the building, the building height itself (75 feet), the cantilevered section over 121 West 15th Street, two geothermal wells, green technology, and much more—and we wanted to be 100% sure we could move forward, full steam ahead, without looking over our shoulders. So we made sure all these specific building points were approved in writing by the DOB.

The architect, Alexander Gendell (his father Stanley Gendell actually was the architect of record, because Alexander had not been licensed yet) worked with us all the way through the process. Alexander—everyone called him Sasha—had also drawn up the interior design of our condo at 121 West 15th Street, as well as the interior of the third floor condo and the staircase of the second floor condo at 121. So we had been working with him for six years already.

Andy Pisani gave us a lot of good advice, too, which Alexander incorporated into the plans. For example, the initial design of the project showed a curved configuration of the top floors and cantilever, which we loved. But Andy advised us that the curved approach would be too radical to get approved initially, what with all the other novel features we were cramming in. He suggested we make the top a more structurally traditional squared shape. Later, we could change the shape to rounded and present an amendment to the project and it shouldn't be a problem to push it through because the square footage would be the same. The main idea was to get the major facets of the plans approved and then revise the exterior design shape later. We followed Andy's advice and, after a six-month process, the plans were finally approved in December 2005.

Whew. Just in time for the holidays.

We thought this review from the DOB was thorough and official, but...

#

At about 10 a.m. on New Year's Day, 2006, our doorbell rang. We were not expecting anyone on the holiday and it was a Sunday morning to boot. We had had a quiet New Year's Eve with the kids, no New York parties, and no craziness. This was the twins' first New Year and Breana had enjoyed staying up late to watch all the Times Square festivities on TV. New Year's Eve was a night when Manhattan became the center of the world and she got a kick out of being part of it. We had a lot to celebrate that year. 2005 had seen a lot of triumphs: the twins were born, the tenants were starting to move on or switch to upstairs rooms, Googolplex had had a good racing season, picking up some silver, and best of all. We had gotten our building plans approved by the DOB. Yes, it had taken six months what with all our unusual features, and no, these weren't the final plans but still, approval felt good and certainly champagne-worthy. But we had chosen to celebrate quietly with our kids. Apple juice and pizza.

There had been times in the wildness of my youth when a ringing doorbell the morning after New Year's Eve might have been cause for consternation, but not this year. Still, I shot Pam a curious glance as I went to answer the bell.

Standing at the door were our neighbors at 125 West 15th Street, Jonathan Gordon and Juniper Tedhams, his sister-in-law and housemate (both look like they just woke up). We knew them only casually and had been cordial to them on the street. This was the first time they'd actually knocked on our door (unfortunately, not the last). As I recall, the conversation went something like this:

"Good morning, Colin," said Jonathan, shuffling his feet uncomfortably. In his hand was a piece of paper.

"Good morning," I replied, "and Happy New Year to you guys."

"Yes, well, that remains to be seen," muttered Juniper.

"Can we talk for a minute?" said Jonathan.

I invited them in and offered them coffee. They demurred. They did not take their coats off, and clearly seemed agitated about something. After a few strained pleasantries I asked them what was on their minds. Jonathan slapped the paper on the table: it was the plans to our new building that DOB had approved just a few weeks earlier.

"What's this?" I asked, though the answer was right in front of my eyes. "I mean, where did you get this?"

"Do you know Robert Boddington?"

Of course I did. Who in the neighborhood didn't? He was the resident parking space watchdog and unofficial garbage can compliance officer. The guy who monitored sound levels at parties and timed the shoveling of sidewalks after snowstorms. You know the type. Keeper of the Sacred Rulebook, self-appointed watchdog of the neighborhood.

Evidently, while the rest of the world had been celebrating New Year's Eve, Mr. Boddington had obtained our building plans from DOB through the Freedom of Information Act. He had then made multiple photocopies and spent the first morning of the New Year slipping them under all my neighbors' doors. Happy Holiday!

"I have to tell you," said Mrs. Tedhams, referring to the plans, "we're pretty surprised and appalled. This doesn't look like something we necessarily want to live next door to."

In a way I didn't blame her. The plans we'd had approved were of a squared cantilever design, which I didn't love either. Juniper was a celebrated interior designer and didn't care for much outside her taste spectrum. I tried to explain the changes we were planning to do and to get my visitors excited about the curved penthouse and green tech we'd be using. I also tried to point out how, with all the publicity we would be getting, and with the high-end price tag of our condos, property values on the whole block would be bound to take a nice leap.

It was as if I were talking to a wooden cigar-store Indian.

"One thing that occurred to us," said Juniper, "was that we might be able to work something out. A contract of sorts."

"Contract?"

"Where you would pay us an agreed-upon up-front fee for our architects and engineers to look over the project, and we would sign off on each aspect of the construction to protect our property."

Ah, so now we were getting at the heart of the matter. They wanted a payoff and approval of my design. Everyone in Manhattan has an angle. "And how much were you thinking this contract would cost me?"

"We were thinking somewhere in the neighborhood of twenty thou."

I politely declined their offer. We soon discovered that they really just wanted us to finish the project so they could start their renovation work. (Which they proceeded to do illegally). As our construction went on, they made their share of 311 calls (the city's anonymous complaint line) and made sure they were a thorn in my side. But, of course, what are neighbors for?

#

I don't know what sparked Mr. Robert Boddington, our soon-to-be arch nemesis to emerge from the woodwork. Actually I do. I failed to pay homage and ask his permission to build on my own property. I also suspect parking space obsession was at the heart of it. A major aspect of our building plan, as you know, was that we were combining two buildings together to make one tax lot with a 40-foot frontage so as to allow for the legal installation of a driveway and garage. As you can imagine, parking spaces are extremely valuable commodities in a city of eight million people with a tiny footprint and a high vertical reach. People kill for parking spaces in Manhattan. It was a moot point in my case because in front of 121 was a fire hydrant so you could not legally park there anyway. I think Boddington was upset that our driveway cut-in was going to subtract a parking space from the neighborhood. (In truth, though, there would be no net loss, because there'd be three fewer neighborhood cars competing for spaces: the three parked in the new garage. So actually we'd be creating three parking spaces in one space.) I don't know what his underlying psychological issue was. But I do know he was obsessed with parking. Boddington had a car of his own that only moved from parking space to parking space on our street, in keeping with the alternate-side-of-the-street parking rules. The car was usually filled with garbage from his apartment and I'm not aware of him ever actually driving it anywhere (that might have forced him to give up his precious parking space), but he sure did park it a lot. Man, did this guy love to park.

It became Boddington's personal mission to defeat my parking garage (and by extension everything else about my new building). One time, in the heat of one of our many arguments on the sidewalk, he wagered $50,000 that I would not get my garage approved. He even went as far to draft up a wager form with the proceeds going to a charity of the winner's choosing.

What a jag-off (God rest his soul).

Mr. Boddington was the self-appointed President of the 15th Street Association (between 6th & 7th Ave). Some years earlier this small neighborhood organization had been formed to fight a zoning variance that would have allowed a department store to be built on the street. This would have caused great disruption to the neighborhood, with trucks double-parking at all hours of the day and night, and freight being loaded and unloaded on our residential street. The group had been successful at stopping the department store and had then disbanded. But on paper it still existed, with Boddington as its president and only member. The man had time on his hands, numerous axes to grind, and multiple bees in his bonnet. I was told he was on paid leave for mental stress (gosh, I can't imagine why) from his job as a financial analyst for some bucket shop in New Jersey. So he had all day to write up twenty-page manifestoes to the Department of Buildings and camp out at the DOB to get people's ears. (I have four of his letters, which I obtained via the Freedom of Information Act, and all I can say about them is Holy Crap.) There is nothing worse than a rebel without a clue who has steady income and unlimited free time.

Defeating my development became his full-time occupation.

Mr. Boddington was an elderly man, in his late 70s, over six feet tall with a balding head. His clothes were typical for a financial analyst: khakis and old dress shirts or t-shirts, wire rim reading glasses. Outdoors, he usually wore a sun cap of the Henry Fonda/On Golden Pond variety. Every Saturday he would canvass the street, carrying a measuring tape, and knock on neighbors' doors if a planter or garbage can was an inch or two too close to the sidewalk or street. He would literally measure it and tell the neighbor of the violation. If, God forbid, the neighbor blew him off, he would jump on the 311 call-in line and make an anonymous complaint on the neighbor. This was his Saturday ritual. Pam and I used to say there is one true, bona fide asshole for every million people, which meant that in Manhattan there were at least eight.

I don't know how all eight of them got to be my neighbors.

Mr Boddington lived at 115½ West 15th Street, about three buildings down on my side of the street. I say "about" three buildings down because his apartment was in the basement of the old carriage house that sat behind the 115 West 15th Street brownstone. To get to Boddington's place you had to walk through the 115 West 15th Street building, then enter a tunnel to his place in the back courtyard. Pam and I went to a backyard barbecue in that courtyard once, invited by another neighbor. He is full of hypocrisy like Ms. Bumble in Oliver Twist.

The really funny thing, given all of Boddington's self-righteous niggling over the fine points of housing and parking law, was that his own apartment was totally illegal. It was completely subterranean, without windows, which is illegal in New York. But the DOB could never get in to see it because he refused to buzz them in when they came calling. Turns out, that's the grand secret to avoiding violation citations from the DOB: don't let them in the door. Boddington's violation has remained unresolved since 2001. That's how the DOB handles cases like this; they just let them remain open until eternity comes and goes.

Ah, Manhattan.

So anyway, we spent over six months resolving the DOB objections and getting our construction plans approved, with driveway, subterranean garage and car turntable, curved balconies on front and back of the building, 75-foot building height, cantilevering roof unit, and geothermal wells. All of these specific points were approved by the department of buildings. But...

Enter Boddington, stage left.

He had our plans re-reviewed twice. Then came Councilwoman Christine Quinn who, on the basis of nothing more than a phone call from a friend of hers who happened to be our neighbor, Juniper Tedhams, at 125 West 15th Street, pulled our building permit for no official reason. A gross and outright abuse of legislative authority, of course, but after this incident several political persons became interested in the development. The plans were moved up to the vice commissioner's desk and then the commissioner's desk for review. So in total our development was re-reviewed five times before it was re-re-re-re-re-approved for construction. All while we were already working on it.

Based on such an extensive and prolonged review process, one would think that our plans would be pretty much written in stone at this point. Surely there would only be minor changes going forward as the building was actually built. But we were soon to discover, to our dismay, that the Department of Buildings has the freedom to completely re-review any building at any time during the construction process, regardless of how far along you've gotten and how much money you have sunk into your project. That is why you have to finish the development as soon as possible after the plans are approved—because once it's built it's a lot harder for them to enforce changes.

Which is what we tried to do, but...

CHAPTER TEN

SCARING UP THE MONEY

❝ *I wanted a perfect ending. Now I've learned, the hard way, that some poems don't rhyme, and some stories don't have a clear beginning, middle and end.*

Gilda Radner

A big part of our story has to do with financing, as do most real estate stories. It was going to take a lot of money to build, Valhalla and Fólkvangr, (the 121-123 West 15th Street Project).

As I've pointed out more than once, financing was not a problem for a homeowner in the early 21st century. We had refinanced our building at 121 numerous times between 1996 and 2003, and each time we were offered more money than we were asking for. Better rates, too. The turn of the millennium was an open bar for banks and homeowners, and closing time was nowhere in sight. We usually worked with an appraiser named Richard Greco in the Bronx, who could work out any number you wanted the appraisal to come in at. Plus he ran two appraisal companies out of the same shop so you could get two different appraisals for each mortgage, which always helped. Richard being an ex- cop and building inspector for the city knew his way around bureaucracy. His big band trumpet player history and on the beat cop attitude made him quite a character from the Da Bronx.

Our building at 121 was a unique place, so finding exact comps (comparative properties that appraisers use to establish a market value) was impossible; you had to find the closest thing and then adjust upward to meet what our building, with all its special amenities and design features, was worth. That left a lot of room for creativity. The banks always took our appraisers' numbers. Why so trusting? Well, trust had nothing to do with it. The numbers looked good on paper and the comps were within a mile of our building, as required, so the bank had no incentive to kick the tires too hard. As far as they were concerned, the larger the loan the better—big ones were easier to bundle in the secondary market. The bank wasn't going to hold the loan anyway; it was just going to make its commission and pass the collection headaches on to the next guy who bought the mortgage bundle that ours was combined with.

So refinancing a home was a breeze. Once you stepped into the big boys' shoes as a developer, though, that was a different story. When you're a builder, the track record of your past developments determines the rates and the mortgages you get. Or whether you get a mortgage at all.

Whole different ball game.

For a new developer without a lengthy track record, it was especially tough. We had only developed one building in the city—121—and while everybody liked our work and the numbers in our proposal played out profitably (over 48% Return on Investment), skepticism was still the order of the day. So we spent the better part of six months getting the numbers together to set up a super-solid construction spreadsheet. This involved getting quotes for building, insuring, manufacturing, and constructing the whole building. Everything from steel-beam manufacturing to porta-potties. Working in our favor was the fact that we had half the total development done. The 121 West 15th Street half of the project was complete and needed only minor painting and renovation to hit the market. (We put in less than $50,000 to make those units sale-ready and they each sold within two weeks of their openings in 2007, and within 2% of their asking price).

Slowly, our budget came together. We got all our subcontractors to give us estimates and then added a 10% fudge factor, which is low by NYC standards. We also threw in a contingency fund just in case.

Here's just a partial list of the contractors that worked on our development:

- Top Penthouse—build and install the top three floors modularly to save time and efficiency

- Plumb Level & Square—dig out the foundation and build the foundation pilings and retaining wall

- Orange County Ironworks LLC (these are the guys from the reality TV show American Chopper)—manufacture the steel frame structure

- All Pro—provide dumpsters for removing construction debris

- Certified Testing Labs—certify all foundation construction

- Contractor's Line & Grade South, LLC—surveying

- Gilsanz Murray Steficek, LLP—structural steel design and foundation engineering

- Quisqueya Construction—demolition and gutting of the building

- Metropolis Group—expediting

- Royal Flush (yup, that's their name)—porta-johns

- Alexander Gendell—architecture

- Goldberg Weprin & Ustin—condo-offering plans and Legal

- HIG Electrical Contractors—remove and shut down power for building and reopen it for new building

...deep breath... And then there was...

- National Reprographics—print copies of all plans and engineering systems

- Aniphase—digital graphic images of our finished project for advertising and website design

- Rohan Classic Iron Work—weld all staircases and railings, which were shipped in from New Orleans

- New Orleans Cast Iron—provide beautiful custom railings and stairs

- Quality Fabrication—weld together all the structural steel

- Consolidated Elevator—manufacture the elevator system

- Solar Innovations—manufacture all the folding glass walls and build the solarium on the top floor

- Interstate Well & Pump—drill the two geothermal wells

- American Custom Lifts—manufacture the hydraulic car lift

- Car Turn—supply the in-ground car turntable in the garage

- Cummins Power— manufacture the natural gas generator for the buildings

- Don Stetner—build real Adirondack wood staircases and railing on back of the 121 West 15th street building

- Sava Tree—remove the trees in the back yard

- Norfast Consulting—plumbing, electrical and geothermal engineering

- Grey Design—custom-built chandeliers and lighting for each condo

- Deltas Testing Labs—drill and test the foundation depth to bedrock and do water tests on the geothermal well

- Rockledge Scaffolding—scaffolding and barricades

- Impact Concrete and Control Inspectors—verify cement is the correct strength and consistency

…And on and on. This list offers just a glimpse of the kind of complexity that went into putting together our building plan. We had literally dozens of additional contractors lined up for things like designing a windmill (would have been first in the city, but DOB didn't have a way to write a permit for it and the insurance company would not insure it—technology once again thwarted by bureaucracy), elevator consulting, painting, carpentry, advertising, insurance; you name it.

As you might imagine, putting a plan like this together was a mind-boggling amount of work. First there was the research and due diligence required just to find these contractors, then we had to play phone tag with them, engage in multiple conversations and exchanges of paperwork with them (bids, quotes, contract specifications, etc.), and then, in most cases, get them out to the site to look at it firsthand. At the same time Pam and I were both working full-time, raising our daughter, and assembling the other pieces of the puzzle, such as dealing with the tenants and doing the design work.

But the good news was, we ended up with a credible and professional construction budget, mapped out in careful detail. The final tally: a paltry $14 Million. But our sales revenues for the finished condos were calculated to be slightly north of $21 Million. So if our numbers were correct—and we had several experts fine-tune and verify them with us—we thought we presented an attractive package for a lender.

We were advised to get a broker to approach banks for financing. Daren Herzberg at Corcoran Group referred us to a good one. The broker contacted over 150 banks on our behalf. We got a few tentative nibbles, but none that would pull the trigger for $14,000,000 in financing. We thought because our project had an appealing and marketable new green design and a relatively small budget by Manhattan building standards we'd find a lender without too much grief. But it turned out our design was too unique and unconventional for the NYC commercial banking market; major banks didn't have any vision and, of course, we didn't have a track record.

But that didn't stop us.

Andy Albstein, our attorney at Goldberg Weprin & Ustin, introduced us to a couple of hard-money lenders, Houlihan-Partners/iCap Reality Advisors, who said they would be willing to lend us some startup capital. Their fund was capped at $4,500,000, but it would be enough to get the project started. Essentially, this was a group of nine people who each put up half a million, knowing that they'd get their money back, with interest, in a fairly short period of time. It was a one-year note and was our introduction to hard money lending. Hard money, in case you are not familiar with the term, is an all-or-nothing commitment. The commitment letter requires a substantial, non-returnable payment—in our case $90,000 (2% mortgage advisor fee)—to get the due diligence done on a tight schedule. Which means you close within two weeks. So you'd better make sure your numbers work or you will lose all the money you put down. Also, the interest rate on the loan was 14%. The loan also covered interest reserve and had stiff penalties for late payments. Oh, and if you don't pay the loan back in a year, they take your building. This was all new to me, but with assurances from Andy we signed the two-page letter of intent and gave these guys a check for $90,000 in March, 2006.

In April we were awarded two loans, one on each property, for a total of $4,500,000 ($1,700,000 and $2,800,000 respectively). This would pay off the old loans on 121 and put some money in our pockets as we started doing the design work and the excavation of the basement of 123 West 15th Street.

We went to work right away paying off the tenants that we had agreements with, digging out the basement, and doing the interior demolition. I immediately went looking for new financing to take us out of this financing.

I went on the Internet, talked to brokers, investors, guys named Vinny, anybody and everybody. In total I contacted over 300 banks, investment funds, brokers, hedge funds, and venture capitalists. I still have the list I put together, three pages long. Major commercial banks just couldn't wrap their heads around the project; it was too complex, too risky. Didn't gel with corporate thinking. They wanted a simple cookie-cutter development (which doesn't really exist in the city), and a track record, because if you have a track record, then presumably you can get it done like you did in the past. We had neither.

So after presenting my proposal to the world over and over again, and getting nowhere, out of the blue this young kid from REIT Management cold-called us looking for loan refinancing clients. It was that kid that brought us to BRT Realty Trust. (He eventually got a $130,000 fee, not bad for a cold call.)

BRT is known as a lender of last resort. As in "You'd be better off doing business with Tony Soprano." If you default with BRT they will take your right arm and your first-born and they will do it legally and quickly. Their contracts are written entirely to protect themselves and to enforce BRT foreclosure. Their loan was "hard money" in more ways than one. In a market of sharks and minnows, BRT was the killer great white from Jaws.

BRT provided a letter of intent, which necessitated a commitment fee of $162,500 and a loan-originating fee of $130,000 from us. So these guys got paid up front. The nearly $300K they required of us to sign off on the deal was about the last of the major funds I had access to, so I was all in. And it wasn't going to be cheap. Interest on the loan was 13%.

Before signing, there was some negotiation on the loan amount and the collateral. I remember spending hours on the phone with Lonnie Halpern (BRT's Vice President and, as it turned out, resident Master of Lies) and the broker while I was getting Googolplex ready for the Newport-Bermuda race. I'm surprised my crew didn't keelhaul me for mental desertion. The sticking point was that BRT wanted my family's life insurance policies and a trust fund my father had set up for me as collateral. I was not okay with that. See, at the end of all this I would still need to refinance and buy my own condo, and if all my collateral was pledged I would not be able to do that. I would have no collateral to refinance with. No exit strategy. When the building was completed I would not be able to buy out my own condo and get out of the mortgage with BRT.

This issue remained at an impasse for a few weeks until we finally agreed to put up $750,000 in collateral, as well as Pam's and my (and my children's) life policies, which had a cash value of $350,000. So we had to set up a collateral account with TD Bank. The collateral account would hold stock worth $750,000. We initially put in $850,000 worth of stock from a trust fund my father had set up—the reason for the extra $100K was that because of fluctuations in the market, the value will change and you do not want a surprise margin call forcing you to put more money in the collateral loan account. TD Bank, however, agreed to specify that only the $750,000 could be used as collateral for this loan. Any excess would remain our funds and BRT would have no right to it. We had them put this in writing and it was signed off by all parties involved. To make this clear: BRT had collateral of

$750,000 held in a TD Bank collateral account in case we defaulted. If we were foreclosed on they would get the $750,000 only; the additional "safety" funds would be released back to my father untouched. This becomes important later. Again, this was spelled out in a binding agreement.

BRT also held my life policies. This meant all my assets were completely invested (my home, the development, my father's trust fund, and my family's life policies) in the project. There was no turning back. But at the end of the day, I needed this loan, so I didn't feel I really had a choice. The first hard money loan was being termed out soon and if I didn't get new funds the project would die.

When you sleep with the devil, make sure you know where the fire escapes are.

The other issue was the cost of the project. Our budget had it at $14,000,000 to complete. BRT didn't want us to lend us that amount; it didn't square with their loan-to-asset ratios and they said their board would never approve it. So they asked us to go over our numbers again and lop $1,000,000 off the total—I still have the email from Lonnie Halpern. Just trim it out. To convince us to do this they verbally assured us that in the end, if we needed more money to complete the project, BRT would be able to come up with it. Lonnie was normal white collar banker in his 40's and really not a bad guy. The nature of the banking business dictated him to always take the advantage of the customer and extort as much money or leverage as possible over their clients.

I did what they wanted; went into the budget and trimmed a million dollars off it, shaving here and clipping there. Of course, I knew it wasn't possible to actually get the project done for a million dollars less; I was just lopping off numbers because they asked me to. It didn't change the reality of what the job would cost by one penny.

I should have learned by that time in my life not to believe verbal promises, no matter how sincerely and convincingly they are made. Lonnie was a master of offering assurances and then ignoring or reversing them when they were not to his advantage. That's how these guys worked. What you agreed to verbally never became what you actually closed with them. My bad—for trusting them and failing to get their verbal agreements in writing. Don't get me wrong, they did lend us the money—$13,000,000—and I did sign the papers and put up money in a collateral account, knowing what was at stake.

But I never could have imagined what would unfold in the near future. Before we get to that…

Another twist BRT threw into the works—ah, the joys of hard money—was that they set up a proviso that any "disbursements from the renovation reserve" (i.e. the loan money) to me would require lien waivers and signed releases, and were limited to two payments a month. So BRT became the project gatekeeper, and if things fell behind schedule or BRT felt their interests were not being addressed, they could shut off the tap. Plus they were entitled to hire overseers at my expense to make sure their interests were being protected. All of this with money I am paying interest on and not available to use.

So it wasn't a matter of, "Here's the money, go build your development," it was, "Once BRT justifies each specific payment, we will release the funds on a case-by-case basis." And if interest payments were in default, all disbursements would cease until the default was cleared up.

What this basically boiled down to, for me, was that I needed someone on site to keep an eye on things; an Owner's Rep who would take care of all the contracts, make sure all my people were doing what they were contracted to do, make sure they were paid, and make sure any contractors' liens were released so that sales of the first set of condos (at 121) could proceed as quickly as possible. This involved a lot of paperwork with the bank, almost daily correspondence. This was where Howard Trueger was to be of use.

Howard had sailed with me the previous season on Googolplex and knew about my Valhalla project from the conversations we'd had while sailing together. He had mentioned to me that he would like to help me in some way. His offer was in the back of my mind, but I hadn't really given it serious thought. In fact I had another acquaintance in mind for the job, one who had much more pertinent experience in the construction industry.

One day Howard and his wife came by the condo to visit us and see the twins, who had been born a few months earlier (while I was in the middle of a yacht race with Howard and the rest of the crew, in fact). The Trueger's brought piggy banks as gifts for the girls and Pam and I gave them the grand tour, telling them the broad beats of our construction saga to date.

A few weeks later Howard and his wife came to the annual Christmas party I throw for the sailing crew. The guests were all the guys who'd sailed on Googolplex that year during the race campaigns, along with their spouses/ girlfriends. The party went on till about 12 or 1 a.m. or so, and the guests were trickling away one by one. I had the sense that Howard and Barbara were deliberately lingering behind. As Howard was talking to Pam in the kitchen, Barbara said to me, a bit awkwardly, "Can I talk to you in private for a minute?"

I felt a little lurch in my chest; I couldn't imagine what Barbara would need to talk to me alone about, but of course I said, "Sure."

We stepped into the bedroom where the guests' coats were being kept and I immediately sensed a change in her mood and intensity level. She wasted no time getting to what was on her mind. As best I recall it:

"I don't know how much Howard has told you," she said, "but he's been out of work for several months now..." Her emotional dam burst and tears came gushing out. "We're way behind in our mortgage and Howard just isn't getting any job offers. If he doesn't find something soon—like now—we are screwed. We're going to lose the house, the car... everything. We're going to be out on the streets, Colin. I don't know what to do."

I wasn't prepared for this but I tried to offer a comforting presence.

Then the other shoe dropped. "He doesn't want me to ask you this, but… I know you need someone to help you with your building project. Howard has some experience managing projects and he's good with the contract side of things. Please, Colin, you've got to help us. Please. I don't know what to do."

Neither did I. But I'm a pushover for a sobbing female. I also have a reputation for helping out friends. Many times I have bent over backward to support them and give them jobs, often to my own detriment, as Pam will attest. Without even thinking, I blurted out, "Sure, Barb sure. Have Howard call me and I'll see what I can do."

Well, Howard called me the next morning, before I could change my mind, and we worked out a contract over the weekend. He was my new Owner's Rep.

Biggest mistake of the project.

The thing is, I knew Howard had had problems as a lawyer and had been suspended from practicing. I should have done a little background digging rather than just trusting him as a friend. In addition to a history of questionable ethics, he had been suspended from his firm for a number of issues, including negligence, failure to do due diligence for his clients, misrepresentations of his actions to his clients, inactivity on clients' cases, and failure to communicate. In essence, for messing up the very things I was hiring him to do for me.

I told you, I have not been accused of being a smart man.

Howard's salary was set at $80,000 a year, working full time on the site, and we set up an office for him. Howard did do some things competently, but his main problem was, he failed to nail things down and follow up. The problems started within the first couple of months. There were details Howard should have been handling but wasn't. I have volumes of daily emails going back and forth with him in an attempt to get items resolved. Damn, if I had to work this hard at managing him, what was the point? Time is money, especially when you borrow at crazy interest rates. I couldn't afford to have issues being left incomplete. Howard's whole job was to be there on site, dealing daily with DOB and contractors and making sure everything was proceeding on schedule, but he wasn't doing his job, at least not at the level of thoroughness required. Pure negligence to the details and follow up.

As I told you early on, he missed the major fraud in the foundation, or possibly received kickbacks to turn a blind eye. I don't believe the latter, really; I don't think he was dishonest per se, just not fully plugged in. Things were always left incomplete, preventing us from moving on to the next step. This is the kiss of death with construction projects in the city; DOB checks the dots on their i's and the crosses on the t's. Howard was a nice guy in his 60's and a good sailor in his time. But in the end his failure to oversee the foundation work led to my downfall. Ultimately, of course, I'm to blame because I put my faith in him and should not have. I was moved by the spirit of the Christmas season and a woman's tears to hire a friend rather than make a sound business decision.

It's never the blacks or the whites, it's the gray areas that get you in trouble. Every single time. Maybe someday I'll learn that.

Anyway, we were funded in August, 2006 with $13,000,000 and the plans were approved, the tenants moved out. Everything was set to go forward as planned. Terrapin Industries LLC, our new corporation, was on its way and the first set of condos at 121 West 15th Street would be on the market in February. When that happened we could pay down the BRT loan by $7,500,000. Eight months from now we would be out of the devil's clutches forever.

At least that was the plan.

CHAPTER ELEVEN

MEET THE CONTRACTORS

66_Courage and perseverance have a magical talisman, before which difficulties disappear and obstacles vanish into air._

John Quincy Adams

Now that we had the financing in place, the project went into high gear. It was such a complicated process, with so many interlacing parts, and so many cross-dependencies, that to try to lay it all out in chronological order, or to explain all the details to you, would make my brain explode, not to mention yours. Each of the contractors provides a story in itself as part of the greater development story, so I will describe a few of them individually here. Then we'll get back to our linear chronology. It's easier this way, believe me. I lived it.

First, a few words about contracting in general, in this unique place called Manhattan. Manhattan contractors are a breed apart. They are accustomed to constructing ridiculously large objects in the busiest city on the planet. Insane things happen routinely in New York construction. Corruption, fines, and payola are part of the game. Just doing bicycle deliveries in Manhattan is an acquired skill, never mind developing real estate. Regular rules don't exist.

When it came to our project, though, we realized there was one rule we could count on. Whenever we described a job to one of our contractors, they would utter the words, "I've never done that before," or "That can't be done." We probably heard these words more than any other phrases in the English language. After each utterance of same, we would explain, demonstrate, and in some cases build scale models to prove to the contractor that the "impossible" task could, in fact, be done. Even then they rarely believed us. In most cases we went through several iterations of the contractors' proposals before we got a final bid and work statement. Why? Because it was crucial that they understood what we were trying to do. Our project was so unique the contractors had to be on the same page as us to make this development work. That is why we only hired contractors that understood the artistic nature of our design and had solid skills and knowledge in their field.

Once the work got rolling in earnest, though, it was my turn to be taken to school. The ol' school of hard knocks. I was about to get a firsthand look at the staggering amount of corruption, incompetence, and downright thievery that lies at the core of Manhattan construction. At first I was incredulous—this can't be the way business is done. But soon it became a matter of "It is what it is"—let's abbreviate that to IIWII, for the sake of keeping this book a manageable length—and trying to keep on top of it. Though I still shake my head over some of the contractor stories we lived through, I reserve the harshest criticism for myself. I can't believe I was naïve enough to expect it to go any differently.

I made an astonishing number of mistakes and learned a boatload of lessons. Topmost among these were:

1.   Never use an architect untested in the ways of Manhattan when you're creating a groundbreaking design in the city.

2.   Don't trust contractors; make them all do a performance bond. Removes any doubt of responsibility.

3.   Never hire a friend who has been disbarred for negligence as your Owner's Rep. Yes, I did that. Earth to Colin.

And of course, the granddaddy of all lessons: "Before embarking on a cutting-edge construction project in Manhattan, undergo a major psychiatric examination."

Oh yeah, and start with more money than you need to complete the work.

My many contractors were only too happy to teach me the thousand other lessons I was ripe to learn. I'll present a few of their stories here. In some cases that will mean getting a little ahead of ourselves, story-wise, but (as I was told over and over by my contractors) we'll get back on track later...

Interstate Well & Pump Co., Inc. Flemington, NJ (Fred Lepore & Fred Lepore Jr.), Samuel Stothoff Co., Inc.

One of the most exciting "green" aspects of our building was to be its use of geothermal energy for heat and cooling. Geothermal energy, as the name implies, uses the heat resources of the earth's core to produce what is for all practical purposes an endless source of renewal energy. If you've ever sat in a hot spring, you've used geothermal energy. Geothermal, however, is virtually unheard of in New York City. There were only eight existing geothermal wells in all of Manhattan at the time we were building. Our use of geothermal alone should have attracted some positive attention to our project. Or, you might say, it should have been a giant red flag for us.

Geothermal requires deep drilling, of course. Interstate Well & Pump, the contractors, were hired to drill a 640-foot-deep well at 123 West 15th Street and a 960-foot-deep well in front of our condo at 121 West 15th Street; a total drilling depth of 1600 feet. Price tag: $184,500. The geothermal wells would pay for themselves within eight years in heating and cooling savings. This would all be distributed through the buildings by use of radiant floor heating and cooling (with additional cooling blowers).

Needless to say, drilling in Manhattan is far from a routine process. It requires approval by DOT (all sidewalks in NYC, again, are regulated by the Department of Transportation), New York State Department of

Environmental Conservation, and the Division of Mineral Resources, as well as permits from the DOB. In our case, neighbors also had to sign off on it to allow trailers and piping on the street. Once the drilling hit its desired depth, the water would need to be analyzed to make sure it had not been polluted by runoff from the streets. (Runoff pollution, of course, is physically impossible at depths of 640 and 960 feet. But the tests had to be done anyway. After all, regulations trump logic.)

The drilling work was done by a father-and-son team. A regular pair of Italian derrick operators complete with the cigars right out of the film "Wildcats" with John Wayne. Deep drilling in the middle of a major city is a real treat, let me tell you. First of all, it's incredibly loud, to borrow a phrase from that Manhattan movie with Sandra Bullock. Especially when you're drilling through bedrock—the sound has nowhere to go, so it echoes and counter-echoes off the buildings and concrete. Water is used as a lubricant for the drill so water is constantly pumped into the well and pushed back out as sludge, which is pumped into a "bladder" in a twenty-ton Dumpster parked on the street. The water then seeps out of the bladder and goes down the street drains. This makes for a lot of water and of course the sewer drains on my street in Chelsea were old. Result? Two brownstones west of my condo got flooded. This was another $5,000 expense and a nice boost in neighbor relations. Which was all we needed.

For two weeks we had this drilling rig that went up forty feet in my front yard of 121 West 15th Street. A plywood covering was built over the building entrance, up to the top of the first floor windows, because of the backwash from the drilling. Two weeks of this incredible noise, wetness, and eyesore, then another two weeks as they did the same in front of 123 West 15th Street. Needless to say, the neighbors were thrilled.

It was around this time that a new wrinkle came into play on the project, one that would persist with other contractors. Interstate Well & Pump started to get violation citations from the city for Dumpsters not being placed in a permitted space. Turned out, Superior Concrete & Masonry, our concrete contractors, had put the Dumpsters in the wrong place and failed to display the permits correctly. These fines are levied for $2500 to $5000, but usually end up being lowered at the hearing to around $500. But here's the rub—you need to know about the hearing to negotiate the penalty. If you miss the hearing you are allowed one second-chance meeting, but if you miss that one the fines are set at maximum.

Well, Interstate got the court notices and did nothing about them, didn't bother mentioning them to me, and then submitted a bill to me later for the full fines. Howard should have been on top of all this, but… Anyway, this was the beginning of a trend of contractors getting violations and presenting the fines to me when it was too late to do anything about them.

The thing was, the violations were usually caused by the contractor and corrected on the spot with the inspector present, yet we still had to go through this time-consuming process with the city. The contractors that caused the violations felt that they should not be responsible for the penalty, so at the end of their jobs they expected me to pay. In order to "persuade" me, they would usually hold something back that I would need in order for their contract to be completed. Essentially they would extort the fine payment from me under the threat of putting a mechanic's lien on the property. Manhattan: the only place where you can pay a contractor a nice six-figure fee and give him two years of work and in the end, he'll still hold you up for a $2500 ransom—for violations that he had caused. Need I say it—IIWII?

The two geothermal wells we drilled still have not been used to this day.

Metropolis Group Inc., NYC (Andy Pisani – DOB expeditor, Wayne Sheppard – DOT expeditor)

Andy had worked with us on 121 West 15th Street (our original six-year project), so we'd known him and relied on him for years.

Andy was well respected in his field and knew the how to get things approved at the DOB. He kept on top of our permit needs and made sure all was done correctly. All permits had to be renewed every 30 days and we needed 12-15 permits at a time—for the scaffolding, the various types of work being done, the materials being used, any after-hour labor variances, etc., etc. These permits usually came in at $50-$150 a shot. Some cost more, some were for longer periods, but they all had to be displayed for the public to see and, of course, for inspectors to review. We would put the approved permits in Ziploc bags to weatherproof them for their 30-day display. This constant cycle of permit renewals went on from 2004-2008 with Andy's help.

Andy also helped with the removal of stop-work orders and any other problems that arose with the DOB, DOT, and OSHA. He was also very influential in minimizing any fines from the DOB.

Wayne Sheppard, Andy's associate, took care of everything related to DOT, which governed the sidewalk and street construction. Another young energetic hard working man who took us through the maze at the DOT to get the correct permits. We needed 17 permits just for the steel erection. These included permits for sidewalk closure, street closure, reserving space for and bringing in a crane, having a compressor on the street, placing material on street, maintaining a fence on the sidewalk, placing containers on the street, and more. Same thing for the geothermal well drilling—permits for everything, very particular and for clearly defined purposes. This is one of the many ways the city of New York gets financed.

Later in the project, Wayne got us a Revocable Consent for the sidewalk radiant-heat ice melting system. This is a system designed to keep the sidewalk one degree above freezing, so that snow melts and ice never forms. That's all it does. For this permit I have to pay the city $4500 a year, because even though I am legally liable for anything that happens on the sidewalk, I don't actually own it, the city does. So I have to pay this massive annual fee just to run a few low-voltage melting wires under the sidewalk (which actually renders it much safer for pedestrians by keeping it ice-free). Only in New York.

Here's the real kicker: I had to make a presentation before the DOT and the city council in Chelsea to prove that my sidewalk ice melting system would not contribute to global warming. Yep. I had a PowerPoint presentation and booklets for the audience—for a forty-foot section of sidewalk, warmed to a mere 33 degrees, only on select days during the coldest few months of the year. This in a city whose concrete and steel basically creates the world's biggest thermal radiator. When we would sail on the Hudson River in the evening, the thermal breeze created by Manhattan's buildings cooling off at the end of the day kept everyone's sails full with a good ten-knot plus wind. But our little sidewalk heater was going to affect global warming? IIWII.

Impact Concrete & Control Inspections, College Point, NY

Every time you pour cement, samples of each pour are put in cylinders. They are tested for compressive strength (Pressure per Square Inch- PSI) to make sure that the cement is at the right PSI for that particular aspect of the construction project. It was Impact's job to do our checking. They also checked all the rebar before the cement was poured to make sure the pieces were all fastened and tied together in the correct fashion.

Cement is an interesting substance. Like muffin batter, it has a short shelf life and has to be poured within a specific time frame. Otherwise it won't have the correct PSI. Remember, this is Manhattan, so if a cement truck gets stuck on a bridge or in a traffic jam the whole load might be spoiled. The contractor doesn't want to eat that cost, so he is tempted to pour the concrete anyway.

That's where inspection comes into play.

I don't know whether Impact fudged our job or not, or to what extent. But they eventually got in trouble for pulling the same type of scam as Certified Testing Labs: falsified testing. What they would do is, instead of testing each and every cylinder as required by law, they would just test one of them (if that) and then use it as a representative sampling. They knew no one looked at each individual cylinder report; people only looked at the summary page. Their summary numbers usually made sense, but if you looked closely you would see that the backup documentation for each cylinder was identical, which is impossible.

They got caught fudging the test data during the construction of the new Yankee Stadium. Some of the poured cement in Yankee Stadium gave way before the project was done. Yes, the floor collapsed, and when that happens on a big, prominent job it opens up an investigation. Heads have to roll. (Or at least it has to look that way on the news. Impact is still in business. IIWII.) Our cylinders were never retested.

Gendell Architecture, Hoboken, NJ (Alexander Gendell, Stanley Gendell)

Sasha Gendell did the complete architectural work for 123 West 15th Street. Nice kid, early thirties, newly married, was designing another building in Hoboken. Had skills and talent. What he didn't have, at the time, was his architect's license, so all of his work had to be submitted through his father Stanley, another good guy, well respected in his field.

The problem was—and this is more on me than on him—this was Sasha's first big project. We liked him because he got our concept and understood our drawings, and after the fourth or fifth attempt to put it on paper he would usually give us what we wanted. So we let our enthusiasm for him cloud our judgment. We were too inexperienced to know that (note to self) you never, never, never hire an inexperienced architect to design an edgy building in Manhattan. We wanted our project to be green, but not that green. An experienced architect, one who'd actually gotten buildings erected in NYC, would have provided credibility to the project. He would have had experience and practical knowledge of the things to avoid. He would have told us ahead of time what to provide to the DOB, rather than playing catch-up all the time with the DOB and the contractors. He would have been on top of the game and driving the project forward. But Sasha was a novice and was learning on the job with a European sense of immediacy or actually lack there being any. Which is death blow on any construction job, when you are always waiting for the architect to provide plans to move forward.

Quotes we got from other architects for this type of job ranged from $500,000 and up. We paid Sasha on a combination contingency/hourly basis, so there was less of an up-front money hit for us. (Second note to self: architecture is not an area where you want to try to "save a few bucks.") Because this was the largest project Sasha had done, he got lost in the details. The combination of his slowness and Howard's blind eye meant I had to spend a ton of time on a daily basis confirming that Sasha had sent documents to the other contractors. He would take his time with everything and the delays were killing me.

In the end Sasha did a good job, but took way too long. Maybe it's me, but when someone asks me for something I give it to them as quickly as possible or I tell them the reason why I can't. I don't say, "I'll get back to you," and leave them hanging indefinitely. Ah well, IIWII.

Norfast Consulting Group Inc. Astoria, Queens (Michelle Norris, Dan Fast)

This was a father and daughter team that designed all the electrical, geothermal, lighting, plumbing, heating, air conditioning, and drainage systems for the building.

Dan did a great job. A little slow, but completely detailed in his work product. He was old school and learned drawing everything out before computers. A father figure full of knowledge. He definitely impressed me. He also sourced the equipment and subcontractors to do the various jobs. The car lift, for example, had to meet many safety requirements. So Dan designed an invisible electric beam that circled the car, 360 degrees, so that no part of the vehicle would be outside the lift going up and down. The parking sequence was: you'd approach the entrance from the street, hit a button on a remote that opened the gates outward across the sidewalk and blocked any pedestrian traffic. Then you'd drive onto the lift. The beam would ensure that everything was inside the car lift and the gate was shut behind the car. Then you'd hit a second button that simultaneously lowered the car and raised another gate behind the car lift so no one could fall into the lift pit as you descended. A third button would then open the garage door below and you could drive into the subterranean garage. Once inside the garage, the door would close with an electric eye to make sure no one was in the way, and the car lift would go back up to street level. Finally you'd drive onto the car turntable and hit a fourth button that would rotate your car 180 degrees so you could back into one of three parking spots. That left you aimed forward to drive out to the street next time you exited.

It was totally cool; the car lift even had an old nautical compass design on it. Dan was great. I'd work with him again any day.

His daughter Michelle? She was another matter. Nothing worse than a girl from Queens with a chip on her shoulder. But IIWII.

Quality Fabrication Inc., Dix Hills NY (Frank Marino, Frank Marino Jr.)

These guys provided the crane and they erected all of the structural steel at 123 West 15th Street, when that part of the job was finally ready to roll. They were in and out in a week. They installed the frame from the foundation up to the fourth floor, where they left platforms for the modular construction that Top Penthouse was going to do.

Frank and Frank were another father and son outfit. Italian, great team, tough and street smart. Their guys were total maniacs, in the best sense of the word. They'd straddle the steel, ride it right off the truck, and weld it in place while it was still being held by the crane. One welder wore a white cowboy hat and rode the steel like a bronco-busting cowboy while he welded. Steel guys are a unique species. Brazenly loony. I guess you have to be, when ten inches of I-beam is all that separates you from a fifty-story swan dive into solid concrete.

The crane operator was amazing. He could blindly deliver a three-ton I-beam using only hand signals from another guy on the roof 100 feet away. No visuals of the beam at all. These guys were a tight crew that had been together for years and did an excellent job. They put on such a show, Breana would set up a lemonade stand across the street when they were working. She could make forty bucks in a few hours selling lemonade at fifty cents a cup. There was always someone curious and thirsty walking by.

Frank got into a face-to-face argument with Boddington one day—it was like Tommy Lasorda going at it with a first-base umpire—and totally ripped him a new one. I'll always love the guy for that.

Boddington believed the No Parking permits the police station gave us were fake. So daily he would go around and remove them. So I would have to put them up again each night. He even went so far as to call the police about the signs. The cops came, I showed them the community relations officer's card I got from the police when I picked up the signs, and they called him and that was that. But that wasn't enough for Boddington. So for a week we did this dance with the No Parking signs. Like I said, a rebel without a clue.

During the steel installation we had to shut down the street, tow cars, and put the No Parking signs up daily at five in the evening for the next day. Then each night we had to deal with Boddington as he turned into Cheech and Chong's Sargent Stadanko over some perceived code violation or another. We had to coordinate the trucks as they waited on 6th Avenue then moved onto 15th Street, where they unloaded the steel as it was erected. There were seven trucks in total, delivering the steel in sequence. We had permits for one week of erection. We had to keep it moving in perfect synchrony, avoid getting our trucks towed, and get them completely unloaded before five p.m. In the end Frank stuck me with three violations too though. IIWII.

The installation of the steel felt like a major turning point for the project.

Contractors say that half of construction is doing the foundation (building the pit) and that once you get out of the pit the rest goes quickly. We hoped that would be true. I was so happy the steel was being installed that I bought beers for the crew at the end of every workday.

The day the steel started going up felt like a major turning point. We finally had the construction accident behind us and the project was moving forward. We had cleared a lot of the major hurdles and you could finally see something of substance going up. It was real now. Exciting. It felt like a vindication of our hard work and perseverance. Now that the steel was going up, there would be no stopping us. There would be no more drastic changes to our DOB plans and we could finally just finish this thing already.

I used to walk around all the girders every day after work and on the weekend. It was a great feeling to finally have something erected, and to see what we had been dreaming of for the past four years finally coming to fruition.

That was the last time we ever had that feeling.

Plumb Level & Square, NYC (Richie Donato—alias Richard Toelk—plus a mason, carpenter, engineer, and 7-9 laborers)

Richie Donato. The pinnacle of my demise. The guy who conned me in the end after befriending me for ten years.

Richie's job, as you know, was to dig out the basement and pour the foundation pilings and the underpinning of the adjacent building. Why did we choose Richie?

We had a long relationship with the guy. He had worked on our building at 121 West 15th Street for six years prior, as an employee of James Krail. Richie had done the excavation and underpinning of both 121 & 119 West 15th Street. (We'd had to underpin the neighboring building, too.) Thanks to Richie's work, we were able to transform a five-foot-high dirt basement with a furnace into a ten-foot-high living area with two bedrooms, a bathroom, and a three-story solarium opening onto the back yard. It came out great. Here is the design plans of the condo.

(You can see more on our web site www.Terrapindesign.net.)

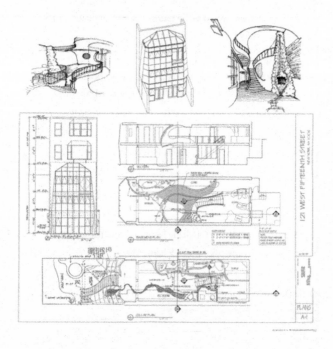

So Richie had been working for us for several years (Jim Krail had gotten out of the business by the time we started the new project). One day he sashayed up to me and said something like, "Hey Asshole can I axe you something?"

"That's Mister Asshole to you," I replied with a perfectly straight face. Richie and I played this kind of game all the time. His was known for his vulgar adjectives and frequency of using them.

Suddenly his expression became serious. "What would you think of me, like, puttin' in a bid on the foundation for the new building?"

"Seriously?" I asked.

"Yeah, I mean, I don't work for Jim no more, so how 'bout if I come in with my own company, give you a quote?"

"Well, you've got the experience, the know-how, the people. You guys did a good job on 121. Why not? If you put in a bid, I'll take a very serious look at it."

"Thanks, asshole. Er... Mister Asshole."

He gave us a quote and we added him to the bid pool as we reached out to several other contractors for quotes. In the meantime we hired Richie to start digging out the basement of 123 west 15th street. We knew for sure he could do that part of the job, since it was identical to 121 West 15th Street, the sister building.

Richie set up Plumb, Level & Square as a company and hired the same workers to dig out the basement of 123 West 15th Street who had dug out 121. That first job had taken a year and 20 twenty-foot Dumpsters full of dirt. All removed by hand. You couldn't bring a backhoe in—not enough space. So it was five guys with pickaxes and shovels filling five-gallon buckets and using a pulley system to haul them to the Dumpster at street level. Shoring up the sides as they dug.

The dirt in the basements of these buildings was laced with river rock and had been compressed for a century and a half, so it was hard work to say the least. The fact that these guys had successfully dug out 121, and had also successfully performed the underpinning of 121 and 119, gave us a lot of trust and confidence in them. We figured 123 would be roughly the same scale of job, at least the digging part.

Richie Donato was the Italian steroid boy with a crew cut in his late 30's. He told us he was a Made Man. He probably was. His old boss Jim Krail was a cleaner for the mob (he disposed of the bodies). When Richie used to wash windows for my partner in the building, Jim Sandino, we used to call him the "Made Maid". He had definitely seen some prison time. Richie couldn't say a sentence without "Fuck" used in it as a noun, verb or adjective. We had to keep the kids away from him during the day because it was constant. He had a habit of always sizing up everybody in case of a fight. I went out drinking with him a few times late in the city and he was the one you wanted to watch your back. Especially, the bar he brought me to. But, he really was just a big kid at heart. I never befriended some many convicts until I started doing construction in Manhattan. Construction industry in the city is littered with ex cons.

An interesting sidetrack was an ironic incident that happened to me during this project. I was called late Friday night by one of the masons that I contracted to do a waterfall in the downstairs bathroom. Jason was a young Puerto Rican semi-professional kick boxer, who usually wore fatigues and a t- shirt on the street. He called me to ask for an advance on the job so he could get away for the weekend. So I met him at the HSBC bank on 14th & 6th Ave at 8pm and got him $500 dollars out of the ATM and gave it to him on the street corner. Thinking nothing about it, I went to the local bodega and got kitty litter and a coke. Then I headed back to my home a block away. I am about to open the gate to my brownstone steps and a car comes screeching around the corner and jumps the curb right next to me. Right out of "Serpico". Out jumps an undercover cop with gun drawn and orders me to spread my legs and put my hands on my head. Then he proceeds to frisk me and asks me where the drugs are. Threatening me with jail time, manhandling me and basically treating me like a convict. It turns out that they observed me handing Jason cash and followed him as well. They made the mistake of grabbing Jason without declaring themselves as Police. Jason thought he was being mugged and flipped the cop onto the ground and ran away until two more cops stopped him. They searched him and was interrogating him the same way. Jason told him what the money was for and they were holding him until they questioned me. So of course they searched me found nothing but kitty litter and a bottle of Coke. They realized our story was the truth. So in embarrassment they let Jason free and apologized to both of us for the error. New York's finest, a little over zealous one might say. IIWII. So then I went inside and told Pam the story, life in the big city I guess. But, stereotypes still exist to these days. Just look at Stop & Frisk stats.

Whenever the local beat cops would visit the site, his crew had a way of instantly disappearing into the shadows, or take a break for lunch—like cockroaches when you turn on a kitchen light. But we felt comfortable with him and he had been working for us for close to a decade without a major problem. Plus, he had recently bought a home in Pennsylvania and had a kid with his girlfriend (okay, she worked in a strip bar, but who am I to judge?). So he seemed to be walking the straight and narrow and was ambitious. This was going to be a big job for him and it would establish him as a legit construction company.

But a tiger never changes his stripes, we found out in the end.

Just to show you the kind of relationship I had with Richie, the first check I gave him to start the work was for $100,000. Just to screw with him, I wrote in the memo field "Sexual Services." Chelsea, you see, is widely known as a gay area. So Richie takes this check without looking at it and goes to the local bank to deposit it. He hands it to the branch manager of the HSBC. The guy looks at the check, looks at Richie. Looks at the check, looks at Richie. Pretty soon he's calling my bank to make sure the check is good. Richie is clueless and finally asks if everything is all right. The manager says the check is fine, but he needs an explanation of the memo.

So I get a call from this guy. "Er, Mr. Rath, this is Mr. Cooper from the branch office of HBSC on 14th Street and 6th Avenue. How are you today?"

"Fine," I say. I already have an inkling where this is headed.

"We received a check for deposit issued by you to one Richard Donato. There is no issue with the funds per se, but as licensed bankers we are under certain obligations to ensure that money is not being exchanged at our bank for illegal purposes."

I wait.

"Would you care to explain the memo on the check?"

"Um, I don't know. Could you remind me what it says?" For some perverse reason, I want to hear him spit it out.

The guy stutters and stumbles and pretends he's reading the phrase for the first time. "Er, looks like, ahem, hmm, I believe it reads, 'sexual... services?'"

So I have to explain that it's a joke and the Italian stallion has to explain that he is not a ho' but a construction company owner.

Richie double-checked his checks from then on. And I got a lecture from the bank.

We received quotes from other contractors and they were all at least double what Richie proposed, so we started getting into serious negotiations with Richie. We talked deadlines, work specs, performance bonds, insurance, etc. It took about three months for Plumb, Level & Square to get an insurance policy that was acceptable to us and our insurance broker, James Milleew. We finally got the insurance and deadlines agreed upon. The problem was the performance bond.

A performance bond is a form of surety that a bank or insurance company issues to guarantee the satisfactory completion of a job by a contractor. In effect, it says that if the contractor fails to deliver, the hirer gets paid a certain amount of money by the issuer of the bond. The cost for this bond was going to be substantial. Seventy-three thousand. Richie didn't want to pay it. I believe our conversation went something like this:

Richie: "I ain't payin' no 73 grand."

Howard: "You have to. It says so in your contract language."

Richie: "I don't give a shit. I ain't payin' no 73 grand."

Me: "I'm not paying it; it's supposed to be part of the contractor's bid."

Richie: "I gave you a rock-bottom price on this job. I ain't paying 73 grand just to make sure I do a job I know I'm going to do. You worried about me finishing the job, you pay the 73 grand."

Milleew: "But it's a standard part of the contracting proce--"

Richie: "I don't give a shit! I ain't payin' no 73 grand."

Howard: "It really is your responsibility, Richie."

Richie: "I ain't payin' no 73 grand."

And round and round. Finally I said something eloquent like, "Fuck it." I decided it wasn't worth going to war over. Richie had completed the last foundation job on time. Or close enough. I wanted to keep good relations with him so I decided not to push for the bond. I chose to believe my contractor would do what he was hired and paid for. After all, there were plenty of built-in incentives for him to do so. If he did this correctly he stood to get lots more work from me; he might even end up as general contractor for the whole project. Plus his contract was for over $800,000. Getting paid this money should be motivation enough for him to get the job done on time. On top of that, all his work had to be verified by Certified Testing Labs and reviewed by Howard and the engineers, and then approved as completed by the BRT people before he got any funds. So there were plenty of checks and balances. No real worries.

Right?

Immediately after I gave him his first major payment for the foundation work, we started having problems. We were supposed to get engineering shop drawings from him, which were to be provided to our structural engineer. The drawings were to show that Richie was building the foundation as the engineers designed it. A cross check, if you will. Well, suddenly nothing was happening. This was weird. Richie had always been prompt. It turned out that he had to fire someone and hire someone new to do the drawing. So the issue was resolved relatively easily, but it was the beginning of the crack that would later become a canyon.

I found out later that Richie, along with a newfound partner/sponsor, had become a part owner of a bar in the Village and had started getting back into cocaine. The old gangster in him began to reemerge with a vengeance.

Richie just couldn't play it straight. One day, for example, all the rebar for the job suddenly showed up. I should have suspected something fishy because, I mean, steel rebar is ordered and delivered on specification; you need different types and strengths depending on the use. Suddenly we have a truckload of higher gauge rebar than we need. This should have been more expensive, but Richie got it for me for the price of the lower gauge stuff. As they say in the

Bronx: it must have "fallen off a truck" somewhere in the tri-state area.

Another thing he did, which I didn't find out about till later, was take all the slate from the back yard of 123 and build himself a nice patio at his home.

You know the old story of the tortoise and the scorpion.

Richie was raised as a conman and didn't know any other way. (And once you get into the ol' yayo, all bets are off anyway.) I offered him a contract that could have transformed him into a profitable businessman, but he couldn't help himself. He threw me under the bus. He could only see the short scam, the quick buck. Once he started going that route, his only hope was to finish the job fast, before his fraud was unearthed. And if the accident hadn't happened it might have worked and no one would have been the wiser. And if the fraud had come to light after the building was built, the insurance company would have covered it. How's that for ironic? Oh well, IIWII.

That's the thing about the city and especially the construction industry. You find out that people you've known for years have been screwing you the whole time. Being two-faced is accepted as normal. It took me a while to digest the fact that you can have friends in NY that you just can't trust on certain matters. I call it the Bright Lights Big City Syndrome. You go out at night and meet people at parties—private parties at friends' homes—and they start talking business. They tell you they have something going on and give you a business card. You call them later and it turns to be complete bullshit. Or you think people are doing you a personal favor, only to realize later that they're getting some kind of kickback. Like this guy we used to know who would get people together at bars for impromptu parties. We thought he was just a really sociable, friendly guy; turned out he was getting a percentage back from the bar.

There was this German guy named Peter on Richie's crew. He was a stonemason who'd done his apprenticeship back in Germany, highly skilled. He still does work for me to this day. Our kids went to the same school and we were friends for years. But he knew about Richie's fraud while it was happening, contributed to it, and said nothing to me.

Richie knew the end was near in September when I began to look for another contractor for the foundation. Did that prompt him to get his act together? No, that prompted him to make a series of obscene, threatening phone calls to me and Howard. A scorpion is a scorpion. We terminated him right after the accident. He was just in over his head, with the scamming and the drugs.

#

Several of my contractors took immediate advantage when my project began to go south in late 2007, mostly by misappropriating funds that were requisitioned for other specific purposes. I understand no one wants to see a big job close, but to illegally steal from a sinking ship is another matter. Take SI, for example…

Solar Innovations-Myerstown, PA

SI's contract was to design, manufacture, and install all the NanaWall-style folding glass walls on the front and back of each floor—a total of 11 wall/doors—as well as the three-story asymmetric solarium on the penthouse. NanaWalls, if you're not familiar with them, are basically glass panels that can slide and fold, accordion-style, to open up an entire wall of a home. Both ends of every floor of 123 west 15th street, as well as one end of the penthouse, were to have NanaWalls to the balconies.

SI was a good team and I looked forward to working with them. But in the end, when I was put into foreclosure, they took us for all they could. Like many of my other contractors, they kept every penny of our deposit and refunded nothing. The total final cost for Solar Innovations' work was

$528,428.04, of which we paid them $260,717.05 and received nothing in return. They kept the product and refunded not cent one. Even though most of the product was never produced. Once I was foreclosed on they doctored up a new invoice and changed one third of that total bill into an engineering charge. That way none of the money could be attributed to materials, etc., for which they might owe us a refund.

They were certainly entitled to some compensation for the work they did do. No argument there. But a quarter of a million dollars? Half the total budget? No one has shame anymore; it's all about the money. Doesn't matter how you get it, just that you get it. I am so fed up with that mindset.

BRT (the lender) didn't care whether SI paid back any of the money or not; they sent out one letter asking for reimbursement from SI. They figured they already had me on the hook for it; they already wrote it off so anything else that came in was gravy. I was the only one who could benefit from getting back unused funds, because it could have helped pay down my debt. IIWII.

I understand not going down with a burning ship, but do you really have to steal all the lifeboats so the survivors can't escape?

Top Penthouse, Union Square, NYC (Padraig Tarrant, Myriam Costillo)

Top Penthouse was the contractor hired to do the modular construction. TP is no longer in business. One of the partners in the firm had a checkered past due to a lawsuit over hazardous waste disposal, but, I reasoned, it's hard to find someone with a totally clean record in the NY construction industry. Everyone gets sued at some point. Overall, we thought TP was on the level.

The plan, again, was to have them build the top three floors in modular fashion at an offsite facility, and then have the units trucked into the city and put together right on the site. This would theoretically save five months' construction time, as well as beaucoup crane time and neighborhood disruption.

Problem I wish I had anticipated: TP was the only game in town and they knew it. Client satisfaction was not their top priority. We spent over eight months just finalizing their contract. I can't tell you how many meetings we had before they would sign on the dotted line. The pattern was: they'd come at us with endless requests for more information (RFIs) and then drag their feet getting back to us. The major lesson here is that the company you hire should really want the job and should be actively seeking your business. The client can't be the one pushing for the contract. Pushing creates resistance. I think that's a law of physics. In construction negotiations it's a recipe for disaster.

The contract finally came in at $1,064,537 for 3608.6 square feet, which translates to roughly $300 a square foot installed. TP agreed to build a total of fifteen modules including the elevator shaft, which consisted of seven block-like modules stacked, that went up the back of the building. Theirs was a complex job for sure, but none of TP's team members—interior designer, architect, project supervisor, subcontracted engineer—seemed to have any sense of urgency about the work. I, on the other hand, had the utmost urgency since I was funding the project.

Inertia, though, turned out to be the least of our problems. To get them to move forward we approved a requisition for the steel order they needed for building.

We gave TP a $190,000 deposit on steel, and only for the steel detailed out in the requisition. When we got foreclosed on (which I'll get into later), BRT asked for the deposit back to lower our balance due. Pat and Myriam, the TP partners, had never ordered the steel, it turned out, and decided to keep the cash or used the credit for other projects. They figured the bank wouldn't go after them for the money since I was already on the hook for it. When the bank did ask for the money, though, all of a sudden a new invoice appeared from TP! It showed expenses in excess of $190,000 for services and storage fees that had never been introduced prior or part of any requisition. In other words, they conjured up a bill so they wouldn't have to refund the money. TP went out of business shortly after that and probably changed their name and moved on to other victims. A common MO for the construction industry.

Back then I didn't know that businesses would rather screw their clients for short-term profit, shut their company down, and start out all over again under a new name than just do the work they're contracted to do. My lesson. We ran into this "business model" more than once during our construction adventures.

The kicker was that HGTV had been contracting with Top Penthouse to film the modular penthouse being built, installed, and finished. This would have been great publicity for the project and our design. And, of course, national publicity for TP. Oh well, IIWII.

That's just a small sampling of our experiences with the dozens of contractors we had to work with. There were many, many more. But I'm getting ahead of myself. Let's get back to the story…

CHAPTER TWELVE

A BAD
FOUNDATION

"_Intellectuals solve problems; geniuses_
prevent them.

Albert Einstein

After the accident with the foundation happened, I remember the day we got
all the engineers, along with Howard and the guys from Superior Concrete
and Masonry (the team we'd hired to replace Richie Donato's gang), sitting
around the table. It only took about two minutes of discussions for Carl from
Superior to deliver the preliminary verdict:

"It's gonna be six months, minimum, before anything can possibly happen
with the actual rebuilding. First you gotta break up the old foundation and
haul it outta there, then you gotta do some test drills, see where we stand,
then you gotta come up with a new foundation design that's gonna work—
and I don't know what the hell that's gonna look like—then you gotta do the
engineering part. Six months, minimum." The other men all stared at me in
silent agreement.

I saw everything fly out the window right then and there. This would
add another year to the project, minimum, and 2007 was perched on our
doorstep, waiting to roll in.

Dark clouds were already massing over Wall Street by this time, if you cared
to look (which most people didn't). The mortgage bubble was growing bigger
and getting ready to burst; it was obvious to anyone paying attention. It wasn't
clear exactly how big the bubble would need to grow first or exactly when
the pop would happen, but a pop was coming soon. The crazy borrowing
and lending frenzy, the insanely inflated real estate values, it couldn't go on

forever. Soon there'd be a lot of people with bubble gum on their faces and I didn't want to be one of them.

In my mind the Stuyvesant Town–Peter Cooper Village sale in the Lower Eastside of Manhattan for $5.4 Billion on October 17, 2006 was the turning point. That happened just a few weeks before our foundation collapsed. The Stuyvesant deal was the pinnacle of banker greed. No matter how you sliced it, it didn't make any fundamental financial sense. The income from the purchased asset couldn't possibly cover the huge mortgage; not even close.

Even a layperson could see the fissures in that one. The Stuyvesant property included 20,000 rent controlled apartments. In order to cover their mortgage the new owners would need to drastically increase the apartment rents, doubling them, plus. I had friends who lived in that place, in apartments passed down from family members, and they were paying less than twenty percent of market rates. It would take the owners fifty years to get all the units empty and to bring them up to market. Meanwhile the whole project would be hemorrhaging money. For decades.

But the banks cheerfully pushed through an aggressive valuation based on an assumption that the rental income would triple by 2011. Really? In Manhattan? What were these guys smoking? It had taken me three years and nearly a million bucks to get nine people out of my rent-controlled building. These guys had 20,000 units! But, as was typical in those days, the banks securitized the mortgage and sold it as mortgage-backed securities before the deal was inked. What did they care whether it worked out or not? It would be someone else's problem to collect on it and manage it. The bankers, lawyers, and brokers had gotten their commissions and that was all that mattered to them.

That deal would later turn into the largest commercial default in America. It had only been freshly inked at the time of our site accident, but I could see the writing on the wall. We were in a horse race against a major economic collapse. So adding another year to our project was a truly frightening proposition.

Not to put too fine a point on it, we were hosed. I knew this deep down inside, but I couldn't give up. What choice did I have? Allow the last three years of hard work and massive expense—vacating and gutting the building, excavating the basement, and underpinning the foundation—to go up in smoke? I would be ruined. I had three kids at this point. Stopping now would mean taking on millions of dollars of dead debt, which might dog me for the rest of my life. So that was not a viable option.

The only way out was a quick fix of the foundation. Time is money, especially when you're carrying financing charges on thirteen million dollars. The sooner we redid the foundation and got the structural steel in, the sooner I could get the units at 123 sold. I had the two condos at 121 finished and ready to hit the market in February. As soon as they were sold, I could pay off half of BRT's loan. Then BRT—or someone—would lend me more money to finish before the bank vault door closed for good.

Okay, so that was our plan. Fix, finance, and finish. Not a great plan, but the only option I realistically had.

But before we did anything, we had to tally up the damage from the accident. And holy crap, there was a lot of it. For starters:

We found out that none of Richie's foundation piers had been built to bedrock (zero out of twelve). I guess that was no surprise. If you're going to falsify one piling, you're going to falsify all of them. But we also learned that the shoring of the rear foundation had been done incorrectly, causing the DOB to designate our neighbor's adjacent property at 125 West 15th Street, rear, uninhabitable until repairs were done. So now we had to deal with our neighbors' building too.

The collateral damages were worse:

DOB shut down the site, put in a partial stop-work order until the foundation was completed, and fined us $35,000. The remediation work on the building would be allowed to proceed provided weekly surveys were sent to the DOB showing that the adjacent buildings had not moved at all during that week's work. This went on for nine months. Contractor's Line and Grade came in to do the survey work to the tune of $27,500.

DOB required the entire back yard to be reinforced with structural steel. We had dug it out completely, to 15 feet below ground level, in order to create underground space for the machine room that would house the elevator machinery and geothermal plant, and PL&S had installed a support wall around the perimeter. When DOB examined this support system they found it insufficient and required us to put in a new one before the owner of neighboring 125 West 15th Street would be allowed to move back into her bedroom. This racked up about $23,000 in engineering and welding costs. Not to mention the cost to our neighbor relations. That was beyond repair.

DOT (Department of Transportation) fined us $10,000, and DEP (Department of Environmental Protection) socked us for another $15,000, but that was negotiated down to $500, thanks to Andy Personi.

OSHA (Occupational Safety and Health Administration) shut down the site for investigation for a week. I negotiated a settlement agreeing to correct the violations, abide by OSHA guidelines, and pay a $15,000 fine. On the good advice of my attorney, I did not officially accept responsibility for the accident since I was going to sue the contractor and submit claims for damages to the insurance companies involved. That was specified in the settlement.

The site had to be clear of materials and debris to make it accessible, and all damaged material had to be removed. Quisqueya Contracting, the guys who had done the floor-by-floor demolition work, agreed to do this for $20,000.

It set me back $18,851 to have Metropolis Group resolve all the permits and fines.

The grade beams (the horizontal structures that distributed the building weight to the pilings) had to be removed since they had no structural support below them going to bedrock. Plus, they were laced with steel rebar making it impossible to drill new pilings through them. The concrete slab that was poured over the grade beams, of course, had to be removed to get at the grade beams. The entire foundation structure had to be completely redesigned, but first, test holes had to be drilled into the bedrock to determine the best new solution. Drilltech Inc.: $16,510.

Then we needed to do the design work done for the new foundation; that cost us over $100K with Mueser Rutledge Consulting Engineers. Plus, we were going to need inspections for the new foundation. And this would not be done, needless to say, by anyone named Richard Zaloum.

Enter Impact to the tune of $8,512.50.

And of course, once the design was complete, the foundation had to be rebuilt again with the completely new design. That was going to be the biggie. Superior Concrete & Masonry came in with a price tag of over a million dollars to do this work (and remember, we'd already paid PL&S $850,000 for the work, all of which was now being flushed down the toilet).

The biggest damages of all had nothing to do with steel or concrete, but with good old-fashioned green. We racked up $1,417,750 in additional financing due to the construction delay and the dramatically increased costs. The building was originally scheduled to be completed in April of 2007 and now we had tacked on at least another year of financing on the remaining $10,700,000 we owed.

So that was that. For a mere $3,000,000, give or take a few pesos, we could, in theory, climb out of this Meteor Crater-sized hole Richie Donato had put us in and soldier forward with this thing.

Meanwhile, we were having frequent meetings with the DOB to get the stop-work order lifted, finishing up the condos at 121 so we could sell them, and getting all the other building components lined up for delayed installation—things like the steel, the car lift, the elevator, and the modular solarium. I was also negotiating a settlement with OSHA. Richie had disappeared completely so I was left to resolve this. We negotiated the fine down from $15,000 to $5,000.

Remediation went on for the rest of 2006 and then we started redesigning the foundation. But at least were making progress again! As for the insurance, that was another matter...

The insurance companies were notified about the accident the same day it happened, November 13, 2006. Once the claim was in, it was investigated by our Builders Risk policy, which was issued by The Hartford with $13,500,000

in coverage, and by Scottsdale Insurance, which was covering Plumb Level & Square for $5,000,000. On December 20th we heard from John Perry at the Hartford that our claim had been denied. The reason? "Deficient or Flawed Workmanship concerning the piers." Hmm, so let me get this straight. They weren't paying for the damages caused by the foundation work because the work was deficient or flawed. Wasn't that the whole reason I had bought the insurance in the first place—in case the work was deficient or flawed? When work is done flawlessly, after all, it tends not to create problems. And when there are problems, well, that tends to be because something was deficient or flawed. Is that not the very thing one is seeking to protect oneself against by buying insurance? Refusing to pay a claim on that basis is like a health insurer refusing to pay your hospital bill because you should have been more careful and not gotten sick.

As for coverage on the old schist wall that fell down, well, since the wall was scheduled to be removed (and therefore wasn't technically part of construction), there was no coverage.

Scottsdale eventually got together (colluded) with Hartford and they jointly stated that since there was no damage to any third party, no damage claim could be honored. In other words, because we caught the problem before we finished the building, they owed us nothing. If we had failed to catch the problem and had gone ahead and built the building, and then it had fallen over (which cantilevered buildings tend to do if not anchored), resulting in monumentally higher damages and injuries, then they would have covered it.

Have to love insurance companies, the greatest Ponzi scheme even invented. Approved and regulated by governments worldwide!

Kind of reminded me of the way the insurance companies tried to stick it to the owner of the World Trade Center in NYC after 9/11. The insurers took the position that the disaster was one incident with two planes, so they could get away with a reduced payout. The owner took the point of view that it was two incidents with two different planes. Both sides had deep pockets and the owner finally won out. I'm sure some actuary somewhere was fired that day.

We had no choice but to sue. On January 10th of '07, we filed a lawsuit against Plumb Level & Square, Richard Donato, Richard Toelk, (same person, Richie turned out to have an alias) Richard Zaloum, Certified Testing Laboratories, Inc., and The Hartford. The suit targeted Hartford for breach of contract. It went after Plumb Level & Square for a number of things, such as fraud; failure to build the supporting piers as required by contract specifications; failure to follow agreed-upon plans; failure to perform in accordance with schedules; and abandoning the site. We also charged Certified Testing Labs with negligence and fraud for falsifying their inspection reports.

All told there were 23 causes of actions for around $1,000,000 each, for a total lawsuit of $22,000,000 against all of the above.

Anyone who has ever been involved in a lawsuit knows that you are looking at 3-5 years, minimum, and a fortune in legal expenses, before anything meaningful occurs (i.e. someone actually writes a check for damages). You spend years dealing with continuances, motions, and counter-motions on both sides and when a judgment is finally delivered, it is immediately appealed. Then it can go on for months or years after that. Insurance companies have deep, deep pockets, courtesy of all the money they extract from their policyholders, so they can fight and delay as long as they want. Which is usually longer than you can wait. They know they can outspend and outlast you, and that's their whole strategy: abide by the Golden Rule (he who has the gold makes the rule).

Scottsdale filed a countersuit against us. After Richie disappeared following the accident, we got a summary judgment against PL&S for $935,000 (the $889,000 we paid him for doing the foundation, plus fines, etc.). Yay. A fat load of good that did us. PL&S had no assets and Richie hid all of his, including himself. Nothing there. So we went after Scottsdale for this and added a few more actions. This was a suit we should have won, hands down. We had all kinds of evidence: forged documents, incriminating video, bogus statements from CTL, photographs, a full engineer's report showing that the work in question had not been performed as CTL stated and approved. We had them by the short and curlies and they knew it. But they had all the time in the world and all the money they needed to keep this thing going and going. They were the Energizer Bunny and we were not. Yup, America has the best legal system money can buy.

The civil lawsuit has become a cost of doing business for many corporations. A company or a wealthy individual can do blatantly illegal, unconscionable things and make crazy profits at the expense of others with only the threat of being sued to stop them. And that's no real threat. If they lose the suit they only have to pay back pennies on the dollar. So what's stopping them? In many cases flirting with a lawsuit is the most profitable route to take. All that's required is that you leave your conscience at the door.

Corporate America figured this out a long time ago. The business model of insurance companies is: collect premiums, deny claims, and fight all suits in court till the other side goes broke. If, God forbid, a natural disaster occurs and you have no choice but to pay a bunch of claims, you can always go to the government for help and/or raise your premiums. The insurance industry is one of the only industries that must remain profitable by government mandate.

So in the end I spent over $150,000 on insurance for the privilege of suing my insurer for failing to cover me for damages that were the exact reason I bought the policy in the first place.

Damn, I should have bought that performance bond.

#

But anyway, the foundation work was now back on track—late, but moving forward—and the lawsuit was underway. Now all we needed was money, and lots of it. We were reaching the budget limits of our allocation categories for each item. For example, we had $1,250,000 budgeted for the foundation and had spent over $850,000 already on PL&S. So we had less than $400,000 left and that was going fast, what with all the remediation costs. Superior's tab alone would be way more than we had left. So the tank was running out of gas, and quickly.

BRT would not let us use funds from another account for the foundation, but—like the noble Hard Money lender they were—they did do us the favor of lending us more money. Not enough to complete the job, of course, but enough to keep the interest reserves pumped up so as to pay them and keep the project inching ahead with one disbursement a month. This way they could keep the project alive enough to sell it in the middle of construction if need be or, if they saw fit, to lend us more money down the road.

BRT lent Terrapin Industries LLC $600,000 on two occasions. They also mandated a minimum sale price on the condos at 123 West 15th Street—the condos had to fetch at least $1550 a square foot or they could not be sold. There's that whole "Lender of Last Resort" thing again.

A main point was this: BRT promised they would lend us a total of $4,700,000 (an additional $3,500,000 on top of the two $600K loans) once we had a general contractor in place and a budget that they approved.

"Said" is the key word here. They did not put it in writing, so we had to take them at their word.

The Godfather had given his promise. I didn't kiss his cheek, but I was sure I would be kissing another part of his anatomy later. You live, you learn.

CHAPTER THIRTEEN

REBUILDING THE FOUNDATION

❝ *By three methods we may learn wisdom: first, by reflection, which is noblest; second, by imitation, which is easiest; and third by experience, which is the bitterest.*

Confucius

Superior took over the foundation contract once the "schist hit the fan" and Richie blew town. Their task was to get the partial stop-work order lifted and do what needed to be done, foundation-wise, so that the steel could be installed ASAP.

Kenny Ferst, President of Superior Concrete & Masonary Corp. was a good guy and had built a solid reputation in his company. He was a big Irish son of a bitch with huge hands that would almost break your fingers when he shook your hand. He and I had already been in discussions about his taking over the project prior to the accident. We'd had several meetings on site and were beginning to talk numbers.

Stupidly, though, I had given Richie Donato one final chance to get his act together and finish the job, because changing contractors would have been a big deal with the bank and because the devil you know…

That decision, needless to say, had cost me dearly.

Anyway, the accident happened and Superior took over. They got all the permits reissued in their name and started doing the remediation to make the work site safe. That was job one. Within a week they had a full crew on the site, underpinning, shoring up the excavation, and breaking up the concrete slab that Richie's gang—the right word for them—had poured. Compressors, jackhammers, a team of seven to nine guys working daily on the site, billing out at $3,400 a day.

The new plan for the foundation was to use 48 mini-caissons, each four inches wide, sunk to a depth of 20 feet. Caissons are hollow tubes reinforced with steel casings, like a pipe, which are then filled in with tied-together rebar and concrete. Caissons make a really strong support, one that also— for reasons I won't try to explain here—helps reduce disruption to nearby buildings and underground structures. This was important because DOB was very concerned about possible shifting in the adjacent buildings. Together these 48 mini-caissons would provide the base for the structural steel.

But first we had to do drilling tests to confirm bedrock depth for all 48 mini-caissons. This of course meant that all the cement that Richie had poured to hide his fraud had to be jack-hammered to pieces and removed. Fortunately, we could use a Bobcat now. We had to cut through 25 inches of concrete slab and pilings filled with rebar; excavate the dirt ramp; create crane allowance to bring in the drill for the mini-caissons; then pour the grade beams again; tie them together; pour the new pilings (using the mini-caissons); build an elevator pit and housekeeping pads for the generator, elevator, and other machines; pour the foundation wall; and also pour an eight-inch floor, with a five-and-a-half-inch-thick bar-reinforced subfloor at the grade beam areas. That's all.

All of this would make the foundation strong enough to support our cantilevered three-story penthouse over 121 West 15th Street.

This meant lots of work for Superior, which you'd think would have made them happy. Unfortunately, after a few months on the job, Carl Marra (Superior's office manager) decided Superior as not making as much as they should from me so they started getting greedy. They decided I should pay them $3000 a week for use of their permits while they and other contractors were working on the job. This was at a time when we were negotiating to have Superior designated as the general contractor for the project (which would have made BRT happy and would have shaken loose the final $3.5 million in financing for us). Instead of going after this multi-million-dollar enlarged contract, Carl, in his infinite wisdom, became hell bent on sucking as much money out of our project as he could and alienating the client (me) and the bank (BRT). He demanded $40,000 just to bid for the general contractor job, which he said he would deduct from the bill if Superior was awarded the contract. Oh, plus he wanted 10% of all contracts I wrote for the project. His terms, of course, were a No Sale with BTR (or with anyone sober). So we had to go back to the drawing board and look for another general contractor. That ate up several more months.

Carl Marra was an older gentleman from Long Island with a dark demeanor, with glasses and a thick Italian accent (like he had been smoking for 3 lifetimes). He threatened and swore whenever confronted on a lie or unable to answer a question about why his company could not make their deadlines. "What are you, calling me a liar?" was one of his favorites. "You questioning my integrity?" "You saying I'm deliberately doing a lousy job?" "You saying me and my guys are not professionals?" He was one of these people who always try to make you look like the offending party whenever you call them on their bullshit. Which was even more amusing because it was all on film— exactly what he agreed to and then later stated to the contrary. Right out of "Goodfellas".

We had several months of weekly meetings that usually peaked with Carl threatening to walk and take his permits with him. Maurice, the project manager, would then calm him down and talk him back to the table. Maurice was the peace keeper, he got a % of my job, so it was to his advantage to make as much as possible out of me.

For these weekly contractor meetings I rented out 147 West 15th Street, a place down the block from us. It was an old nightclub that had gone bust; supposedly Johnny Depp was part owner. Anyway, the building owner couldn't sell it or rent it so we made a deal and rented it for six months as a showroom for the condos for sale and a meeting place. We had weekly

Monday meetings with everyone on the project. I have many hours on video of arguments with contractors who had failed to do what they said they would do the week before and of Carl Marra blustering and storming out of the room. Classic stuff.

The bottom line is that the Superior guys came on strong at the beginning and were doing a great job, but in the end they sort of crapped out. They weren't motivated to do a good job, on time and on budget. I was just a cash cow for them to milk. Like many of the other contractors we encountered, they failed to realize that doing the job right and on schedule would benefit them by getting them more work through referrals. BRT, for example, told me outright that they would work with Superior on other projects if they did a good job, and I passed that along to the Superior guys. But they took no apparent pride in their work; it was just how much more can we soak this for before the funds dry up?

Superior began falling behind on completing the foundation, which kept pushing back the steel installation.

I was getting nervous.

BRT was getting nervous.

The housing market was getting nervous.

The banks were losing their liquidity.

Tick, tick, tick.

While all this was happening, the natural gas generator I ordered for the building had to be shipped, so I sent it to Better Lists' warehouse in Connecticut. This was a huge machine that cost $50,000 and could power both buildings in a power outage. (When I later needed to fire-sale it, I discovered it had almost no resale value. Why? The market was glutted with generators from all the other buildings that had gone belly up. I ended up selling it for $5,000 online and was happy to get that.)

The car lift had to be shipped, too, because there was no space for it at the manufacturing plant and it was too big for my warehouse in Connecticut. So we had it shipped to a site Superior had on Long Island, then tarped it up to protect it from the elements. I never actually laid eyes on it. Maurice said it was impressive. Superior charged us $2100 to unload it, even though the need to store it was caused by Superior's own failure to stay on schedule. Another example of contractors milking the cow from both ends.

The original schedule called for many of the major building components to be ready in time for the steel installation, because as soon as the steel was up these components had to be quickly put in place. Walls were the next step after steel. Once the walls were in place you would have to reopen them to bring in any major components in after that. A lot of added work and expense. So everything had to fit together like a well-timed puzzle; otherwise you'd be doing things over and spending more money. Once one item fell behind, the whole chain would go down like dominos.

Well, that's exactly what was happening. Everything was falling behind. We started getting Saturday work permits to get caught up, which added a lot of cost and overtime. But we had to get the steel in ASAP. Meanwhile, Superior was getting less and less reliable and giving us more and more attitude as they slapped on more and more unnecessary charges.

One example of their worsening attitude was the way they dealt with Contractors Line & Grade, the company we hired to do the weekly surveying required for the DOB. As I mentioned, every week we had to have the two adjacent buildings, 125 and 121 West 15th Street, surveyed to make sure they did not shift at all during our construction. CL&G did a great job. The problem was, they were punctual and Howard Trueger and Maurice (of

Superior) were not. Over the months I got multiple messages that CL&G had shown up to do a survey at 7 a.m., waited for someone to meet them, and then finally left. CL&G had to charge for these missed work sessions, of course, and I passed the charges on to Superior since they had been the ones to set up the meeting.

I am sure Superior found a way to tack them back onto my bill.

This started to become a recurring theme: when contracts went bad as a result of failure to do the job correctly or missing deadlines or needing to redo work, the contractor at fault would inflate the bill by adding on charges that were not previously discussed. It was obvious that these new line items were invented purely to cover their loss from their own mistake.

Our original contract with Superior to rebuild the foundation and do the mini-caissons was for $428,245.00. Then came the change orders, seven of them altogether, that ballooned the bill up by over a million dollars by the time Superior left the job. This wasn't all Superior's fault, but their foot-dragging and general sense of entitlement and uncooperativeness certainly compounded the problems. Which was all I needed.

CHAPTER FOURTEEN

PR WOES -AND MORE

❝ *I have never found, in a long experience...*
that criticism is ever inhibited by ignorance.

Harold MacMillan

In March of 2007, we decided it would be a good idea to create a record of the project for posterity. I had been doing some video and photography of the ongoing work since 2003, but now, with the project shifting into high gear, we were beginning to sense that this might be a subject worthy of a professional documentary. A movie. Why not?

The seeds of the idea actually grew out of a series of social get-togethers, years earlier, when Pam and I had been working on our first building. Everyone acquainted with us at the time knew we were doing a major renovation on our brownstone. Pam and I were managing the construction crews and designing interiors in addition to concentrating on kids, careers, our online art gallery, yacht racing, and life. Living La Vida Loca. We became the "colorful local developers" with a story to tell. Anyone who has done any renovation work always like to hear about the problems and experiences of others, especially if those problems make their own look tiny. So Pam and I would tell our latest stories to anyone who asked. In the eyes of others, we were living a never-ending drama, which only grew more convoluted, funny, and dramatic over time.

I guess our story was unique because our project (the 121 building) was exceptional — the two-story waterfall, the brass fire pole, the laminated comic-book wallpaper, the scale replica of the Yangtze River built into the living room floor. Our challenges on that project were inherently interesting and strange. Add to that the colorful cast of contractors, like Richie, the "made man" who was allegedly a hit man, Jim who was a "cleaner" for the Mob (the guy who disposed of bodies), and the electrician who drove a hearse with personalized Elvis plates and lost his wife to a local witch. Usually after being handed a drink at a party, Pam and I would launch into our latest chapter. A crowd would form around us. At each party more and more people gathered. It was like the narrative sequence of scenes in the movie Six Degrees of Separation.

Several friends began to suggest that we should film what we were doing on our new development project, especially since 123 West 15th Street looked to be even more interesting than 121. Essentially, it was going to be the first green construction of its kind in Manhattan. So it seemed bound to stir up a whole new spate of stories. Why not capture it on film?

One day, at a school party for my daughter, we ran into a parent of one of my daughter's classmates who had a company called Cactus Three. They made documentary films. (Her company later consulted on the production of the Academy-Award-winning film The Cove.) We started having conversations. She told us about the costs and processes involved in making a successful documentary and coordinated the assembling of a film crew to shoot it. Soon we were off to the races. Hollywood here we came.

Well, maybe Sundance wouldn't be bad.

Basically, the idea behind shooting a documentary is that you turn on a camera and record everything. If you do this long enough and consistently enough, sooner or later drama will happen. Once you have it all filmed you then spend a small fortune editing the miles of footage and making it into a film. So we hired our first cameraman and issued an announcement to all our contractors that they were now officially movie stars and had to sign waivers. The next five years were filmed, photographed, and documented.

Our hope was that the film would generate some buzz and—just maybe— some revenue that could help compensate for some of our staggering losses.

But the nature of documentaries is that you can't control what happens once the shooting begins. If you could, they would be propaganda, not documentaries.

The film crew interviewed everyone they could find who was connected in any way with the project—my old partner Jim Sandino, some of our old tenants, DOB reps, every contractor who worked for us. They also recorded all the contractors' meetings and a lot of the construction work. Needless to say, not everyone had great things to say about me—hey there, Jim Sandino—or about the building. After all, it was a cutting-edge design, which offended the sensibilities of many who felt that Manhattan neighborhoods should stick to their historically prevalent styles. (I am sympathetic to this point of view, but if we stuck slavishly to this mentality, there'd be no innovation in architecture and ninety percent of the fascinating structures in the world would never have been built.)

The worst thing to come of the documentary filming was that I created a bully pulpit for Robert Boddington. As you know, he'd been a thorn in our side for some time already, but as soon as the film crew started interviewing him, he became a star, at least in his own mind. Whereas before he had been content to remain the unpopular neighborhood curmudgeon who measured trash can placements and monitored parking spaces, now he began to fancy himself a media personality. He began to thrive on the attention, but also, I think, he began to see how publicity could help him further his cause. He invited the crew over to his apartment, where they recorded hours and hours of private seminars on The World of Building, According to Bob. The more he talked, the more comfortable he became as the center of attention.

This emboldened him, I believe, to speak more openly against us to the neighbors. Thanks in large part to his efforts, we began to feel hated in the neighborhood. People would cross the street to avoid us. As for Boddington himself, he would confront me on the street any chance he got. He would crowd my personal space and yell in my face, just begging for me to shove or hit him, so that he would have something to "get me" on. One time he began shouting at my kids—Breana was 5 and the twins were 2 at the time!—when they were just walking down the street with their nanny. I think the man was seriously unbalanced. Diagnosable. What kind of man yells at a nanny with children under 6 years old?

Pam even went as far as to make her special seven-layer brownies to give to Boddington to try to cool the situation down a bit. She stayed up late one night baking and when she saw him walk past the next morning (having just come back, incidentally, from a meeting with the Deputy Commissioner Max Lee at DOB to discuss my project), she ran out with the brownies as a peace offering. The first thing out of this guy's mouth was" Are they poisoned?" Pam is an emotional woman and was in tears trying to reason with him to back off her children and family. He would have nothing to do with it and stated that he was going to do everything in his power to destroy our project. He proceeded to lecture her on his meeting with the DOB and how he was satisfied that their latest review would force us to build a building more to his liking. The penthouse solarium, he said, would be a blight to the neighborhood and he would not allow it.

Keep in mind that the solarium, even if you considered it a blight, would not be visible from the street since it would be set back 15 feet at the 60-foot level. He did offer to stop his continued attacks on us with the DOB in exchange for our allowing him to review our project on an ongoing basis.

I had warned Pam that nothing positive would come out of her peacemaking efforts. But, Pam has a good heart and tries to see the best in everyone. Me? I always figure what goes around comes around. Sooner or later Boddington would get his. But when I saw him strut off leaving Pam standing there in tears with the tray of brownies in her hand, I wanted to kill the guy.

The DOB continued to field his endless complaints and to give him their ear. Of particular concern to Boddington was the height of our building. He was obsessed with the idea that our building was too tall for the neighborhood and made constant reference to the so-called Sliver Law to buttress his point.

At issue, supposedly, was the idea that our top floor would obstruct sky views from the street, even though we showed, over and over again that because of the 15-foot setback, as required by its zoning lot, it would be completely invisible from the street and would not affect the so-called "sky exposure plane." Below is the zoning law for my zoning district R8B form the DOB handbook.

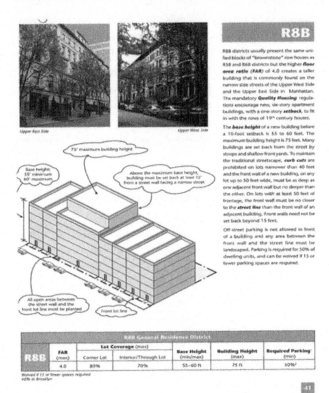

I guess DOB had no choice but to listen to him, given the fact that his letters were extremely detailed and clearly born of the type of mind that thrives on making trouble. Still, it amazes me that one noisy citizen with a vendetta can make an entire city department jump to his demands and that approvals given to a construction developer can be continually re-audited and re-re-audited, even when the project is in mid-development. How can anyone build anything if one disgruntled individual can force endless work stoppages and redesigns of previously DOB approved plans, with no regard to the costs to the developer? Don't property owners have civil rights too?

Boddington wasn't our only enemy. Keep in mind that Manhattan is populated by eight million people daily. When cell-phone cameras became commonplace, everybody and their mother instantly became a reporter. Now throw in Mayor Bloomberg's introduction of 311 calls, where anybody can now anonymously submit a complaint about anything. It doesn't matter if it's true or false; the Department of Buildings has to record it and send out an inspector to check out the complaint. So if you want to be a pain in the ass to any building project, you go to the nearest public phone and make a 311 call. Or file a fake story online. No repercussions, no personal responsibility.

We had several neighbors who used this system liberally. So we became intimately familiar with every building inspector; their numbers populated our cell phones. There were 64 official complaints registered against our project over the years. Many of these were instigated by 311 calls from Boddington, or, in the early stages, from our perpetually angry tenant Mr. Harrison. All of the complaints were quickly resolved or dismissed. But as they say, it's a death of a thousand cuts. If you are constantly getting reapproved you're not moving forward.

Even before we started filming, our building plans had been re-reviewed two additional times for a total of three reviews/re-approvals.

In April of 2007, our plans were reviewed yet again, and approved again. But then, two months later councilwoman Quinn met with the DOB yet again and this time the DOB reviewed 33 objections ranging from the merely nitpicking, like requiring us to plant a tree in front of 123 West 15th Street; to the needlessly annoying, like asking us to prove that the grade of the back yard had been returned to its original slope after our excavation; to the truly problematic, like lowering the height of the building. This was almost two years after the initial plans had been approved and re-approved three times, and now all of our building components were manufactured and ready to be installed. This time we had to meet with the Commissioner and Deputy Commissioner of the Department of Buildings because political interest had now been attracted to our project. It took several months to get the plans approved again and signed off by the Commissioner again.

#

As we were scrambling to get through this latest round of DOB setbacks, a New York Times feature article about our project was set in motion by the people at the Corcoran Group. We were looking forward to its publication. Some good press would give us a badly needed shot in the arm.

The Corcoran Group, if you recall, had come aboard early in the project to contribute to the design and to help us understand the high-end condo market. We were building something new in Manhattan and wanted to make sure the market would buy our "green dream" idea. Daren Herzberg and Brian Babst of Corcoran were experts on this stuff and they were great with marketing and PR.

Daren was instrumental in getting the Times interview set up for us. It had taken a long time and a lot of phone conversations with the newspaper to build up enough traction to make it happen, but finally we were ready to roll. The Times article was to be a huge PR boost for our green building and would provide a launching pad for our development company. We were naïve enough to believe that because so many people loved our design ideas and because we were pushing the boundaries of green technology, that we would be supported by the press, especially by a paper like the Times which is generally thought to pretty liberal. You have to remember that this was before LEED certification and green design became the norm. Ours was a cutting edge project; no one at that time was committing themselves so radically to green design. Our design was both revolutionary and sustainable, certainly worthy of some press.

Finally the day arrived when journalist Fred Bernstein came to meet with us in our condo. Typical NY Times reporter in his 30's, dressed in jeans and a button down shirt. Right out of "All the president's Men". What we had hoped for—and were told—was that the article would be about our green design and geothermal energy system, as well as our fresh architectural ideas. We met with Bernstein for about 3-4 hours, with the kids crawling around, and conversed enthusiastically about our design. He asked the right kinds of questions and seemed genuinely interested and supportive.

Then the conservation veered off into what the neighbors thought and any problems we might be having in that regard. We were straightforward about the run-ins we'd had with neighbors, and about Boddington's objections to the building.

We thought the interview had gone well and felt very positive about it. The Times ran a great picture and (online) slide show about our condo on its website in anticipation of the feature article. So it should have been a great bump for exposure and sales. We were excited and anxious.

#

On the morning of June 17, 2007, a Sunday, I was awoken at around 7 a.m. by the ringing of the phone.

"Yeah?" I croaked. I don't do polysyllabic till after coffee.

"Is this Colin Rath?" asked the caller.

"Speaking."

"Oh, hi. I'd like to take this opportunity to tell you what a f***in' piece of sh** you are. You and your little trophy wife ought to be ashamed of yourself.

Kicking low-income people out of their apartments so you can build some piece-of-sh** eyesore that only Broadway stars and ad executives can afford. You're exactly what's wrong with this city today. F*** you and the BMW you rode in on."

It wasn't the first "fan" call we'd ever received so I didn't think too much of it. But then, about ten minutes later, the phone rang again. Different caller ID.

"Colin Rath," I answered, more cautiously this time, wandering out to the kitchen so as not to wake Pam.

"Yeah, why don't you go f*** yourself." Click.

Two "go f*** yourself"s in one ten-minute period. Wow. That was unusual. I had no sooner gotten back to the bedroom when the phone rang a third time. Another new number. I picked up again, more than a little hesitantly.

"May I speak to Colin Rath?"

I opted for silence this time.

"Oh, nothing to say for yourself? That's a first. This is Chuck from Albany and I hope your little Chelsea sh**hole burns to the ground." I switched the phone to speaker and walked back to the bedroom so Pam could hear. "In fact," continued the caller, "I know a couple of guys who might be able to make that happen." The caller then let loose with a stream of "words I never heard in the Bible," as Paul Simon would say, capping it off with, "Have a nice day, asshole."

"That's the third one in a row," I told Pam.

Just then, Breana came stumbling into our bedroom, rubbing sleep from her eyes. "Who was that, Daddy?"

"Nobody, honey, nobody at all."

A few seconds later the twins, Nerina and Meriel, wandered in, too, seeming to pick up on the anxiety and weirdness in the air. Pam and I each picked one of them up to comfort them. "Is everything okay?" Breana asked.

"Everything's fine, Sweetie," I said, but the expression on my face told a different story.

"The article!" said Pam. "Today's the day the article's supposed to come out."

Of course! I rushed out to the front door to grab our copy of the Sunday Times and quickly flipped to the Real Estate section. I spotted the article, "Green Home of Their Dreams" and started to read hungrily. The first words were, "Matthew Mathosian couldn't afford to buy a house on Long Island…" Huh? Matthew Mathosian? It took me a few seconds to realize this article wasn't about us; it was about someone else building a green home. I flipped to the beginning of the Real Estate section and there I saw a huge photo of our building design, right above the fold. I spotted the headline for the real article about us and I knew we were in trouble. It was entitled, "Not in My Front Yard," by Fred Bernstein. (http://www.nytimes.com/2007/06/17/realestate/17cov.html)

The first three paragraphs were all about Robert Boddington and his heroic crusade to save his neighborhood from the "alien pod" that was soon to be built there. Boddington! I spat the name out like Jerry Seinfeld saying, "Newman!" Boddington had managed to grab himself a new soapbox to stand on! (He actually made copies of the article and kept them with him to hand out to people like a personal press kit—I guess copyright laws didn't apply to him either.)

The more I read, the more appalled I was. The slant of the article made us seem like clueless, self-absorbed uber-yuppies who had heartlessly and unceremoniously kicked out a bunch of low-income tenants to build an architectural monstrosity to be sold to other rich a-holes. At least that's how I read it. And given the repeated ringing of our phone that morning I guessed I wasn't the only one who was reading it that way.

How naive we had been, once again. The writer had made us think he was on our side. But the press is all about selling papers, and I guess stories about a nice successful couple with three cute daughters designing a green building don't sell a lot of papers. New Yorkers want slander, gossip, and class warfare. A story about a "rich" (we weren't) couple throwing poor people out of their homes (we didn't) to build a building the neighborhood hates (many people actually loved it)—well now, that plays out much better for the paper and reporter. It doesn't matter if an article is true or not anymore. The paper can always retract it a week later in a little blurb no one reads. As someone in the construction trades once told me, "It's easier to do what you want and apologize later than to do the right thing."

When the phone rang for about the sixth time in the space of half an hour, I was about to rip the cord out of the wall, but I noticed a vaguely familiar name on the caller ID.

"Hello?" I said.

The caller identified herself. She was a Terrapin client who had agreed in principle to buying one of the duplexes at 123 West 15th Street. At our full offering price. She had left for Switzerland the previous weekend and was staying at a spa there. As best I can recall the conversation:

"Mr. Rath," she said, "I read the Times article online this morning."

"Nice pictures, huh?" I said, a bit uncomfortably. "I thought the writer was a bit—"

"I can't get involved in a building with a shady past," she interrupted.

"Shady past? What do you mean?" I was genuinely confused. The article hadn't even mentioned the old WWI brothel stuff. Anyway, that was a hundred years ago.

"What you and your wife did to those tenants. Kicking them out on the street. Terrible."

"We went through that process very carefully and respectfully and paid those people a lot of money to relocate."

"Relocate? The term you used in the article was 'get rid of them.' I'm in a sensitive position socially and professionally," she said. "I can't afford to be associated with this kind of a story. I am withdrawing my purchase offer."

Crap.

The twins felt the same way about Mr. Berstein's article and proceeded to tear it apart the on the living room floor. They had a blast throwing the paper around and ripping it into little pieces. We videoed it.

CBS news did a story on us and the Curbed.com website began running exposés on our project. These were just awful. At least the Times had had to provide some facts in its story, but in online journalism there is no semblance of truth-telling. It's whatever the "reporter" (i.e. guy or gal with a camera phone) decides to make up on the spot. Nothing checked, nothing verified. Online, anyone can say anything without recrimination, using aliases or blogger names. Kind of like in politics, some people figure if they repeat what they say enough times it will be considered fact. And sadly, it works.

I've come to realize that there is no unbiased and reliable news source in the

US anymore. Period. It's all hearsay, hysteria, and opinion masquerading as fact. The days of journalistic integrity have gone the way of the slide ruler.

After the article came out, things went from bad to worse in the neighborhood. Signs of protest began popping up. Copies of the article started appearing on telephone poles. At night people spray-painted awful messages on the front of our construction site;

I had to pre-screen the neighborhood before I would let my daughter step outside in the morning. Neighbors who had been cordial refused to talk to us anymore. The insulting and threatening calls got so bad we needed to get an unlisted number. You could feel the anger toward us in the air like a visceral thing. I suddenly no longer felt safe letting my kids out of the house without the nanny, or even letting them play in the back yard. We had lived on the block since 1996 and had made many friends there. All of a sudden that all changed. Rumors and innuendos about us ran rampant. There were a few good friends who knew better and continued the friendship, but the majority of the people on the block—who didn't know us at all—allowed their ignorance to sway them to hostility.

I'm sure the Times article also threw fuel on the fire of the local politicians who had it out for us. I'm sure it all got back to the DOB (Boddington took care of that), which now felt additional public pressure to squash our project.

When DOB got back to us with their response to the latest round of 33 complaints, courtesy of the Boddington, it was a good news/bad news scenario. The good news: we had the green light (for the fifth time) to go ahead and build. The bad news: it was going to cost us. Hugely. We were forced to lower the total building height to 60 feet, which meant losing an entire floor of the building, remove the 1st floor front balcony, and redesign back staircase on the exterior of the building. The tragicomic irony of it all was, if DOB had just given us this response from the start, we would have scratched the cantilevered penthouse early on, which would have meant we wouldn't have had to anchor the building in bedrock, which would have meant we could have gone with a simple foundation design, which would have meant the foundation would have been done right the first time—for millions of dollars less—which would have meant Ace would never have been injured and the condos would be finished by now, purchased, and occupied. And we'd be comfortably in the black, planning our round-the-world sailing adventure.

But now we were going to have to find a way to pull the project out of the fire once again and make it profitable—with one less floor to sell and another huge new wave of expenses tacked on. Many of the building components—structural steel, NanaWalls, solarium, elevator parts, etc.—had already been manufactured according to the old design, and of course DOB doesn't give you any refunds for this kind of stuff. They just say, "Change your plans again. Sorry." Government looking out for us, right? Always watching at any rate.

Because we'd lost a floor, we had to have our structural engineers, Gilsanz Murray Steficek, redesign the steel for about $20,000. Gendell Architecture had to completely redesign the penthouse. Norfast Engineering had to redo the engineering for the top floors. Severude Engineering had to rework the structure of the modular units. Solar Innovations had to redesign the solarium and doors and remove some doors already made. Consolidated Elevator was brought back in to change the elevator construction. Top Penthouse came back to redo its design. Et cetera, et cetera. You can imagine the kind of tally this ran into.

The thing that killed me was that we had gone out of our way to present extremely thorough plans at the beginning, so we could get all this stuff pre-approved before we started building. We couldn't have done it more by-the-book if we tried. But we were never told that approved plans could be reviewed and unapproved at any time. Mr. Boddington gamed the DOB and the DOB bowed to his pain-in-the-assness. His only qualification was that he was persistent and had a grudge against me. That's all it takes to have the DOB ruin someone's life or at least derail. .

We were not a big job, as Manhattan projects go, and we didn't have any clout. Otherwise we would have just sued Boddington and everyone who had signed off on our plans at the DOB and then broken their contracts. I did have my attorney write Boddington one "cease and desist" letter, but I didn't have the budget, or the time, to sue everyone. I was too busy racing to get my building finished and sell it before the housing market crashed.

After the fifth design change was signed off by the Commissioner of DOB, she gave us her personal assurance that this was the absolute end of the review process. I'd like to say we were relieved, but by then I'd learned that verbal assurances were worth about as much as Bruce Dern's prize ticket in Nebraska. If DOB could re-review us five times, what was to stop them from doing it a sixth time?

Despite all our setbacks, though, the steel went up that summer. A building was actually taking form! We had turned the corner.

Maybe...

CHAPTER FIFTEEN

CREDIT MARKET COLLAPSES

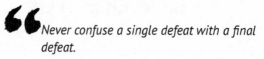

Never confuse a single defeat with a final defeat.

F. Scott Fitzgerald

I saw the writing on the wall sooner than most others. I knew that the lending frenzy in America was getting truly insane and that something had to give. It's an old trading truism that if the world thinks the market can go nowhere but up, the pendulum has to shift.

Newer and grander real estate deals were being thrown together in Manhattan every week and the banks were just rubber-stamping them. Anyone could see that this type of cavalierness would ultimately lead to disaster. I was hoping to finish and sell my development before that happened. I was praying the real estate market would party for one more year before its parents came home. Please, God, one more year. I needed to keep my financing intact to finish the project and then I needed to sell my condos quickly and for a good price as soon as they were finished. If the market didn't hold up, I was sunk.

The housing market, at that time, was still believed to be invincible. It could only expand, the thinking went. The U.S. government didn't even have a mechanism for reporting negative housing growth. A negative number had never been recorded and the government's computer program didn't have the capability to report one. The whole Main Street world assumed expansion was a given. It would go on forever. The banks were selling that idea, too, with the full might of Madison Avenue behind them—radio, television, direct mail. Begging people to borrow their money. I personally would get five refinancing offers a week in the mail in the years from 2003 to 2007, not to mention cold calls. Foreign investors were flocking to the United

States to invest in real estate and real estate-related securities like never before. Banks were handing out so-called "liar loans" that required little or no documentation. One percent down, quick turnaround. Bam, here's your check.

U.S. households increased their debt-to-disposable income from 77% in 1990 to 127% at the end of 2007, much of this increase being mortgage related. Consumers took close to $5 trillion out of home equity between 2001-2005. The banks knew—and the market makers knew for sure—that the housing boom wouldn't last much longer, but they wanted to extract every last penny they could before it fizzled. Wall Street firms were playing both sides against each other and making sure they had a parachute for themselves when the plane ran out of gas. They were selling mortgage-based securities on one side and taking out derivatives on the other side against the position they had just sold. So in essence they were betting against their own customers without the customer's knowledge and without telling the customer their true opinion of the market. Isn't that why the customer had come to them in the first place—for their market knowledge? No conflict of interest there. Scumbags.

If you were reading the signs—and I sure was—you knew the dike was cracking. As I mentioned earlier, the Stuyvesant Town-Peter Cooper Village deal had sounded alarm bells up and down my nervous system.

On our project, though, we thought we had gotten over the hump. The structural steel had gone up. Yes, there had been a work stoppage in the middle of that job, prompted by your friend and mine (the self-appointed King of 15th Street), but that had only set us back a week. We seemed to be on track and had only one more hurdle to cross in order to access the final $3,500,000.00 in funding from BRT. That hurdle was that we needed to get a new general contractor for the project, approved by BRT. Once that happened, it should be all green lights from that point on. We had delivery dates for the car lift, the Nana Wall system and Solarium were getting ready to be installed, Top Penthouse had taken its delivery of steel (or so we thought since we'd invoiced BRT for the steel order.) IIWII . Fingers crossed, we should be finished construction by April 2008. We even had some interest in sales too; one of the simplex condos was close to a contract already. All was looking promising.

If the market would just hang on.

But BRT had put a clause in our mortgage that "Lender shall not make any disbursement for Work unless the Lender has determined that the amount of the Reserve that will remain will be sufficient to complete the work." Based on that language, BRT stopped disbursing funds to us after the steel was erected. The reason? They wanted to approve our new budget and get the new work-completion loan signed before cutting lose any more of our money. (They continued to pay their rep, Alan Garry, as well as their environmental engineers, out of my funds during this shutoff time, to the tune of over $30,000. Only a slight contradiction there.)

We were working hard to get BRT what it wanted. Meanwhile, the construction needed to keep moving forward or we were going to be screwed with our contractors. So that meant I had to keep things going with my own funds. I started scrambling to sell our most valuable possessions, figuring we could always buy them back or replace them once the funding was resolved. I sold a 16th century Dutch grandfather clock to a dealer for $30,000; I had bought it during my flush days for $155,000. We started selling off the art collection we had amassed through the running of our online art gallery.

We had acquired a modest collection over the years—30-plus paintings totaling in value just north of $400,000. These were mostly oil paintings we'd obtained at "wholesale" prices from artists we represented when we ran the gallery. We sold a few at auction at Sotheby's and a few auction houses in New Orleans and San Francisco. But the market for art had become diluted. Everyone was selling, so there was a glut on the market. Auction houses were full of stuff. Art and antiques, I guess, are the first things you sell when times get tough. Still, the paintings had to go. Painful as it was, Pam reminded me that we could start collecting art again, if we wanted, once we got through this rough patch.

For me Pam's belief was the key to getting through this: she believed in me and she believed in the project. Sure, we were down and it sure as hell looked like we were out, but deep inside we knew that eventually we would climb out of this and be back on our way. Now was the time to liquidate everything and save our development. Do what needed to be done.

Selling everything actually turned out to be a positive move for us. We both realized that we had become too caught up in consumerism. We had too much stuff and weren't hungry like we used to be. We needed to consolidate and take a hard look at what we really needed. After all, if we were going to live on a boat someday, we needed to learn how to live lean. And if we wanted to teach our kids that experience and togetherness were more important than material things, we needed to put our money where our mouths were. We sold on eBay, Craigslist, and at tag sales just to get rid of stuff and drum up cash.

Everything was getting less than twenty cents on the dollar. All my income from work was pouring straight down the open mouth of the project. We were doing anything we could to raise cash. At one point we rented out 121 West 15th Street, the whole building, to Playgirl Magazine for a photo shoot. We needed to have someone on site to make sure the building was not abused, so our Nanny Camilla spent the evening with twelve naked male models as they got photographed in bathtubs of milk and on fireplace mantles. She got to see firsthand what a fluffer does. The photos made the centerfold of the magazine, September issue. We got $7000 for a twelve-hour shoot. Not bad. It went right to the contractors.

I managed to keep the project going for a while at partial strength, but I didn't have enough to cover the monthly interest payment of $74,000 a month. I was working frantically on setting up the final budget for finishing the building, but there were pieces of that puzzle that took time. BRT did accept our recommendation for a new general contractor, Garadice Inc., so that was good news. Garadice had a good record in the city and was finishing up a condo project on the Upper East Side. John Maguire, the president of Garadice, knew his stuff and had done a dozen buildings in Manhattan and Brooklyn. John was a straight shooter and worked with me for months trying to get this together with BRT. He came in with a budget of $2,924,000, a scheduled starting date in July of '07, and a completion date of St. Patrick's Day, 2008—April at the latest. Which, for those keeping track, was before the big crash. So had BRT left well enough alone we would have been sold and out of the project in time.

Needless to say, that's not what happened.

BRT was getting antsy. Extremely so. I was talking to them three or four times a day via email and telephone. I was on the verge of three months past due on the mortgage, with $190,415.81 in undisbursed repair reserves that were due to me. Lonnie Halprin of BRT would not distribute any of our money or let us use it for interest payments until the contract for the new loan was in place, which would add $3,500,000 to my funding. The BRT people weren't willing to be flexible at all, even though I had I paid them back over $7 million less than six months earlier. In fact I handed BRT $250,000 the exact same day "the letter" arrived…

On July 21, 2007 Pam called me in tears saying that we had received a summons notifying us that BRT was foreclosing on 123 West 15th Street and on our home condo, which we had put up as collateral.

Oh, and BRT also intended to grab the $750,000 in the collateral loan account.

I got on the phone and speed-dialed BRT. The gist of our chat went like this:

"Lonnie Halprin, please?"

"Colin," boomed Lonnie in a jovial tone, as if I'd just called to wish him a

Happy Birthday. "And how are we this fine day?"

"Fine? I just got the notice!"

"Oh, right, right, that. So how can I help you?"

"I thought we were all working together here in good faith," I explained. "Why didn't you tell me you were planning to foreclose? Give me a heads-up?"

"Listen, don't worry about it," he replied. "We still intend to do the next round of financing with you."

"You've got a peculiar way of showing it."

"The foreclosure notice is really just a formality, to keep our friends in Legal happy. Everything is still moving forward. The notice won't be reported to the credit agencies and we'll hold off on liquidating the collateral account until we've signed the new loan."

"Really?" I asked, taking a deep breath. "Whew. Then I shouldn't worry about this?"

"Not until there's something to worry about. But I don't see that happening."

I hung up, feeling as if a hundred-pound weight had been lifted off my chest. Of course I didn't get any of Lonnie's promises in writing, just his word. But what choice did I have but to accept it? I needed BRT's financing to fight on and finish this development.

When foreclosure hit, though, Superior slapped a mechanic's lien on the project, which killed any future financing with BRT or anybody. We came to loggerheads with Superior as to what they'd completed and had not completed. I finally signed a personal note for $81,630.12 and gave them $20,000 to release the lien, which they did. Fucking Carl.

But then the Bear Sterns implosion happened in late July, 2007. Bear Sterns' two big hedge funds were invested in real estate securities that derived their value from mortgages, and when those mortgages ran into unexpected trouble (i.e. being worthless scraps of paper since they were based on mortgages that were now defaulting, big surprise there), their value plummeted. This left investors demanding that money be added to those hedge funds to provide additional capital, but, alas, there was no money to be had. Bear Sterns informed its investors that its two huge hedge funds had "effectively no value" and on July 31, they officially went bankrupt. The first of the Wall Street house of cards to fall.

Suddenly, in late summer of '07, all the development projects in the city got a bad case of shriveled balls. They were all being revalued and developers were being asked to put more money and/or collateral into their projects as appraisers began lowering their property value drastically. The general mortgage market was still puttering along with the help of Mortgage-Backed Securities (MBSs) but now at a small percentage of its height of $600 Billion in 2006.

The mentality of the shadow market had changed. The shadow market is the secondary market made up of large financial institutions (AIG, Bear Sterns, Morgan Stanley, Bank of America, Chase Bank, etc.) and Hedge funds that trade in MBSs and derivatives. A derivative is a financial instrument that essentially allows you to wage a bet against a large financial institution (insurance companies, investment companies) or against interest rates or markets, without having to really own anything. All you need is someone to take the other side of the bet. Usually some palooka not in the know. Real shaky stuff.

Even shakier: all these transactions are off the balance sheets. Off the books means exactly what it says: it does not get included in the profit and loss statements of the business that deals in these instruments. This is because the credit rating agencies issued them as a Triple A security, certifying that they were risk-free (they could never lose value according to Moody's, and S & P, so why would you put them on your books?) So, for example, a business, say AIG, sells derivatives that insure that $1 trillion of mortgages will not default. These instruments don't show up on their financial reports, and because they're sold in the shadow market, they are constantly sold and resold to anyone in the world and are virtually impossible to re-organize via bankruptcy. So when AIG's derivatives are called—that is, the owner presents them for payment because the mortgages are now in default—AIG suddenly has a huge debt and no way to pay it off. Because it has sold a hundred times more than the value of the company.

Governments, for example the Unites States Government, cannot allow such financial giants to go bankrupt. Why? Because the financial system would implode. All over the whole world financial markets would shut down, because no one would know if the other party was stable or was holding so much off-the-balance-sheet crap that they were insolvent also. So now the situation is that no one knows anyone's true financial status because there could be something off the balance sheets that is not being disclosed. Crazy. By the way, this market is totally unregulated and still operates this way today—even after this whole mess the banks got us into. Also, this market is larger now so watch out for wave two to hit harder in the future.

The best part of the credit market collapse is that the banks invented Mortgage Backed Securities and derivatives and then exploited the general public to the saturation point by selling mortgages to anyone who could sign their name to a piece of paper. Then, when it all went to crap, the banks received a bailout from the government because these financial instruments were designed in such a way that they could not be unraveled to find the end owner. To top it off, the banks then used their bailout money to speculate in the stock market and financial market to make unprecedented profits while lending very little of the new money to the public, which was the prime reason for the bailout. Add in the fact all the financial houses had their losses covered at 100 cents on the dollar and all their executives received their annual bonuses all paid by the taxpayers money. Now is congress looking out for it's citizens or big business? You decide.

But, I'm getting ahead of myself. That stuff mostly happened in 2008,

In 2007 I was still trying to keep BRT happy.

Well, you guessed it. BRT didn't wait for our new loan contract, as they verbally promised they would. On August 17, 2007 they liquidated our collateral loan account of $750,000. There went three generations of Rath family savings in one click of a mouse button. Some of those stocks had been bought by my grandfather back in Montreal in the early 1900s.

But, BRT wasn't satisfied with the $750K and tried to take the rest of our collateral account, which had an additional $105,000 in it (to cover fluctuations in the market so as to avoid margin calls). This additional money was designated by TD bank as not collateralized. In other words, BRT wasn't supposed to touch it. But Terrapin Industries (me) had to sue BRT to stop any further liquidation of the collateral loan account and our life insurance policies.

#

The year 2007 had started off with great promise as we climbed out of the foundation hole and erected our steel, but it ended with the whole world imploding on us.

I continued to keep the project going at a snail's pace with my own money. At the same time, I began looking for new financing in a dwindling market of sharks and trying to negotiate a settlement with BRT to buy back my project, while redoing the condo offering plan according to the new and fifth re-approval of our design. Mentally and emotionally, I was sinking into quicksand.

Meanwhile, every creditor involved in the project—and with me personally— came crawling out of the woodwork looking for money...

CHAPTER SIXTEEN

THE JUGGLING ACT

> **"** *It isn't necessary to imagine the world ending in fire or ice – there are two other possibilities: one is paperwork, and the other is nostalgia.*
>
> Frank Zappa

We were in survival mode now—under an all-out assault from creditors and just trying to get through it with as little added damage as possible.

We no longer had any funding, of course, and the building was under foreclosure, as well as our home. So we made the business decision to default on our business debt. After all, the business, Terrapin Industries, was insolvent. Any business accounting course would tell you to do the same in our situation. But credit card companies don't provide credit to businesses, they provide credit to members of businesses. You are the underlying creditor, so they come after you personally. Or, I should say, they sell you out to someone else (a collection agency) who comes after you personally.

In the early 2000s creditors, credit cards, and business accounts were all dumping their debt on collection agencies. These collection people are like hyenas circling a carcass. Pure scavengers. Some of them would call literally ten times a day. It got so bad in the end of 2007 that we got rid of our home phone and answering machine because it would fill up in one day with collection agencies' messages. So we just relied on cell phones and didn't take calls from unknown or unwanted numbers.

The thing you have to realize is that once a bank or business sells your debt to a collection agency, they write it off and you usually get a 1099 that is reported to the IRS as income for you or your business. Prior to selling the debt the bank adds in every possible fee allowed by the small print. This inflates the debt to as high as possible, which allows them to lower on paper the embarrassingly high profits they make from things like fees from free checking. (Free checking is the gold mine of commercial banking; take a look at any profit and loss statement for any bank and you will see why.) But I digress. The reason they send you a 1099 is basically logical: they've taken the loss, therefore you've realized a gain. But aha, not so simple. The bank then sells your debt, bundled together with other debt from the bank, to a collection agency. The bank makes money selling its bad debt, maybe 20-50 cents on the dollar, depending on how recently the debt was defaulted on, and at this point actually nets out, or close to it.

Now you have a collection agency that adds more fees onto your already fee-loaded debt and starts to contact you for payment. The collection agency's only real leverage is your desire to protect your credit rating. So they work you, using any trick in the book. They want you to feel responsible and remorseful, so that you will pay any portion of the debt right now—right now when they have you on the phone. The collection agency keeps all of what you pay on the debt—none of it goes to the original creditor—and the bigger payment you make the more they get. The debt is already written off and you have been taxed on the gains, but that had nothing to do with the collection agency. They own your debt now, just like in mobster movies. They will promise you deep discounts, anything to get you to crack open your wallet, because all the money they recoup goes directly to them.

After about six months the collection agency will sell your debt at a reduced price, with another bundle of debt, to another collection agency, and the process will start all over again. Again the debt is increased at the new agency, and so on, and so on.

I have three fat three-ring binders full of all these collection letters. I had over 26 outstanding debts with Terrapin Industries. A few of them are still kicking around and have made it to their seventh collection agency. These are the truly rabid hyenas. These clowns call with "special offers" that are 50% off the markup of the original debt. Sure, pal. Whatever you say. They write you bi-weekly and call you 24/7. This has been going on with us now for over six years. But all of that the debt we defaulted on was business debt and the business was insolvent. Period. Still, that doesn't stop these people. It's pointless talking to them; they just try to make you feel guilty and scared and try to extract a promise or a partial payment. Remember, though, our credit card bills were in the tens and hundreds of thousands dollars. We had been using these accounts to finance the building and then repaying them with the BRT funding as it came in. And that funding no longer existed. No matter how many times I try to explain the whole "can't get blood from a stone" thing, they keep coming at me. I know my credit will never fully recover from this.

During the time following the foreclosure we continued to try to put our hands on as much cash as possible to keep the development going while we desperately searched for new completion financing. Even though we'd been given notice of foreclosure we were still trying to salvage this thing. Which meant I had to keep doing things like: resolve issues with the DOB in order to stay in good standing with them, get the condo offering with the new layout approved again by the commissioner, maintain all the permits for the ongoing work, keep all the contractors happy so they wouldn't put mechanics' liens on the project (I had $1,691,349.12 worth of open contracts with these guys), and keep working with our lawyers to move forward on our lawsuit. Not easy to do with negative funds. But it was essential that we keep the project viable so we would have a credible package to show to financers and, most important, so I could put all three units at 123 West 15th Street into the hands of buyers. And we had to get it done before the foreclosure became final and the property went up for auction.

If I could keep all these balls up in the air, I figured financing would happen. Somehow. Eventually. So juggle I did, in addition to working full time so my family could have money to live on.

Problem was, at the end of 2007 refinancing was to next impossible, and after the credit crash of 2008 it was undoable without divine intercession. Our track record made things even tougher. In the beginning we'd had no track record, but now we had a totally schizophrenic one—Project A, the 121 West 15th Street condos, was a raging success and sold out within a week of hitting the market, at offering prices; Project B, 123 West 15th Street, was a total disaster.

If we didn't get financing, we were on the streets, totally screwed. And soon. I'd known this was a possibility from the start, but I felt I had done my homework and had anticipated most of the potential obstacles. The one thing I hadn't foreseen was outright fraud. I guess getting conned didn't occur to me because it seems like such a dumb business model.

Speaking of cons...

With the whole financial world in flux, every developer was in some sort of trouble with their financers. This brought into the credit market a whole new breed of cutthroats. Some of them were just looking to make a high return on an investment. After all, when it comes to real estate in Manhattan, supply will always be limited and demand will always be strong, so anyone with foresight could see that it was only a matter of time before prices would go back to where they were in 2006. (In fact, we are surpassing those prices per square foot as I write this in 2014.) So there emerged these new investors, banks, and hedge funds that had some cash and wanted to buy at the bottom of the market. Get the lowest price on a property and sit on it or develop it and wait for the market to come back. No crime there; that's good old-fashioned capitalism.

Then there was another group—land sharks, I called them. They promised you the world as financers. But their only interest was in getting your non-refundable commitment fee, then skipping off to the Azores. I even met with a few who flew into the city just to do the meet-and-greet and get their check from me. They knew you were desperate for a loan and were hoping beyond hope that their commitment was real. You'd spend three or four weeks sending them documents and comps on the property while they supposedly did their due diligence. Then they'd send you a letter of intent and a loan commitment letter and ask for the fee up front. You'd scrape together the funds somehow and wire them to their bank—it could be anywhere from $1000 to $20,000— and that was the last you'd hear from them. You'd stop receiving emails and your calls were not returned, and eventually you'd realize what had happened. Knock, knock. Candygram. You'd been eaten by a land shark.

I went through over 350 different funders from venture capitalists to mortgage brokers to banks to hedge funds to angel investors. You name it, I tried it. I put my proposal out there on HardMoney-Lenders.com, the Breadstreet Investors Union, Go4Funding.com. I had several different application emails cued up, with all the needed attachments, plus a three-ring binder ready to overnight to anybody who wanted a hard copy. It had 378 pages of pictures, along with all the contracts, permits, plans, comps—everything anyone needed to do due diligence on my development (it helped that I ran a printing company).

I started making the rounds of every possible lender I could think of, getting referrals from friends on Wall Street and in local banks. Hell, I even asked my brother who is a real-estate mogul in Stamford, Connecticut. He gave me a quick brush-off that eventually led to a family confrontation I'll talk about later.

The first funders to offer financing were Titan Capital from Westport, Connecticut. They gave us a commitment letter, which we used as an attempt to hold off BRT's foreclosure. Cost: $5,000. The letter didn't mean anything unless we actually closed, of course, but the idea was to keep BRT, especially Lonnie, off my back while I got the financing put together. It worked for a couple of weeks and then no loan materialized. These guys are worse than bankers, which I didn't think was possible.

I tried everything I could think of to negotiate with BRT. I spent months trying to lower the price BRT would accept for the property. We tried partial payouts. We asked BRT if they would accept a subordinate position in the

216 • **It What It Is** • A True Manhattan Real Estate Nightmare with a Silver Lining

development, but they wouldn't do more than $1Million. We came just short of asking them if they wanted us to smuggle a planeload of heroin across the border for them. At the same time we were forced submit motions and cross motions, get stays of foreclosure, submit requests for summary judgments on the property, etc. We were able to tie them up until November 2008 while I tried to get financing together. It was a delicate dance of negotiating a settlement while delaying their foreclosure process. My legal counsel really out did themselves on my behalf and kept my family alive and sheltered. .

The key to this all was that the real estate market in New York—and everywhere, for that matter—was in free fall. You could not get reliable comps for any property; appraisers were low-balling everything because there were no true market sales around, only foreclosure sales. So nobody—not financiers, not banks—would pull the trigger to finance unless the property was an absolute steal. We would get really close and get promises of financing only to find out at the last minute that the appraisal came in too low to cover the financing. I spent every waking hour filling out loan applications and sending documents, along with my 378-page binder, to financiers all around the world. We would send out all our stuff, talk to the finance representatives for about three weeks, answer all their questions, physically meet with them at the site, and thirty days later find out there was no deal.

I always had three or four financing possibilities going at any one time, and each one took about two to three months of daily emails, calls, and updates to see if they would fly, fizzle, or fold. In all I got over 35 letters of intent, with loan commitments, asking for funds from me. Not one of them came through. Not one.

It was incredibly draining on both Pam and me. At the same time we were running up legal bills in the hundreds of thousands defending our property and the assets of my father. It was a very trying time. Pam and I had some serious discussions about D-Day plans of action. But somehow we hung in.

You may say that the problem was not the market but my project, that it was a losing proposition. But I really don't believe that. It was a unique project, true, and required special financing as such. But the numbers were solid, and there were lots of people who really loved our designs. There was profit to be made in all the financing matrixes I used and based on all the property comparisons I had gotten from the Corcoran Group. So I really don't think I was deluded about the project itself. Besides, I wasn't exactly alone in this financial mess. Millions of other property owners were treading water like me.

The problem was simply that the market was freezing cold and no one wanted to get back into it just yet. Everyone was waiting for bottom to be hit. All the money was sitting on the sidelines, watching the game from afar while End-of-Days scenarios were being flashed on the news. Brokers were trying to sell packages to investors and though many of them were still kicking the tires, few were putting up cash. Big Money could sense what was happening in the financial market and its hair was turning white with fear. Anyone who was still offering financing for real estate developments was asking for huge cash reserves for worst-case scenarios.

So I was fighting frantically to be the last development refinanced before the collapse. Every day I read about other developments getting shuttered—left as holes in the ground with scaffolds around them in hopes that funding would eventually reappear. And many of these were straightforward, mainstream projects, not green-dream, eco-luxury units with geothermal wells.

Here are some highlights (lowlights) of our financing voyage:

In autumn of 2007 we spent four months with East Coast Financing as they did due diligence for a loan of $11,850,000. We finally got a commitment letter that I paid $15,000 for. All looked good until an outside appraiser from Florida came in with an appraisal that was too low. Luckily, East Coast did refund our commitment fee 60 days later, because they failed to do their due diligence within 20 days as stated on the commitment. Whew. Got my money back, but still no loan.

In December of '07 TCRM gave us a loan Commitment for $8,000,000, along with $3,000,000 structured as an equity partnership. We paid $5,000 for the commitment letter and they never came through. No surprise there, I was dealing with Russians.

From January to March of '08, we had a commitment from Eastern Savings Bank for $12,000,000. We paid $13,000 for this. The appraisal came up short for the Loan-to-Value, so—again luckily for us—they returned our deposit.

In late March of '08 we were working on one of the more creative deals, with a group called Bairnsdale International. These guys were throwing some really crazy numbers around. The deal involved doing something called a Collateral Enhancement Commitment. Here's a bit of the verbiage from that deal:

...You are seeking to borrow $15,000,000.00 USD, but will eventually obtain a loan commitment for ($15,000,000.00 USD x 4 = or roughly $60,000,000.00 USD). Approximately 69% (at current prices) of this amount ($41,400,000.00 USD) will be used by the lending institution and the trust or securities firm to purchase the zero coupon financial paper which, at maturity (ten years), covers and repays the principal amount of the loan ($60,000,000.00 USD). Approximately 6% ($3,600,000.00 USD) of the amount is used to pay fees and commissions, and the balance which is approximately 25% ($15,000,000.00 USD) is the cash "fall-out" to the Applicant. These amounts will be adjusted according to market requirements...

Understand that? Me either. To get this puppy rolling, they wanted an up-front "collateral enhancement commitment fee" of $175,000, a "loan commitment fee" of $125,000, and a "Professional Executive Consulting

Retainer" of $28,600. Needless to say, this one didn't work out either.

In April through June of '08 we worked on another colorful deal, this one from AA Funding Solutions. It was for $15 million to be paid in two draws. It involved a Cost of Loan Fee of $700K due upon approval of the formal loan commitment, a Facilitators Fee of $300,000, and a Brokers Fee of $450,000. Oh, and an up-front retainer fee of $50,000. The good part, though, was that I didn't have to put up the $50,000. They had a hard money lender in Florida, Thomas Bonds, who agreed to write up a short term loan for $50,000 that I would pay back at closing. But here's the kicker: he would get a 100% return on his loan whether it closed or not. I swear, I walked into Goodfellas on this one. This guy hounded me for six months for payment of the $50,000 profit he was due on a deal that never happened and I had no proof that the funds were ever put up.

On June 10th, 2008, we got BRT to agree to accept $5,850,000 for a buyout of the property and I had a commitment letter that looked feasible. The fine print? We had ten days to close or we would be found in default and our foreclosure would be sped up from three months to five weeks. Big mistake taking this deal. But I wasn't exactly flush with options. This deal got totally messed because the lender thought Terrapin Industries was being foreclosed on at 121 West 15th Street and they didn't want to risk lending to an entity that was in foreclosure. But Terrapin Industries was only the loan originator, not the borrower, and that was why it was listed in the foreclosure documents. We corrected the documents and sent BRT letters legally showing the Terrapin was not the owner. But time was now running out, and BRT would only give us a 15-day extension if we put down an immediate $750,000 deposit.

Andy Albstein, my attorney, lent me the funds to do the deal. (He actually did this twice and I repaid him twice.) Andy is a great guy, one in a million. He did more for me and my family than anyone else ever in my life. I will always be forever in his debt for the enormity of his generosity. He saved my home and my family. But on June 23, the deal was officially blown dead (on that same day I got an email from Goodfella Tom Bonds stating he would take

$38,500.00 for his $50K payment and call it even).

When the BRT deal fell through I got a voicemail from my good friend Lonnie Halprin saying something like:

"Hey there, Colin, just wanted to let you know, we've got no choice now but to put your foreclosure on the fast track. We warned you about that one. Have a nice day."

The foreclosure process was expedited, as BRT had threatened. My desperation went into high gear. Over the next several weeks, I got involved with a couple more land sharks. One wanted $12,000 for a commitment letter; I managed to get out of paying that one before it fell apart, but I did get stuck for $15 grand on another deal. Still no funding. Now foreclosure was coming at us like a runaway freight train.

As D-Day approached we decided to play poker; that was our only move. On August 8 of '08 one of my lawyers notified BRT that they should release my life insurance policies and any claims on the "extra" $105,000 in the collateral loan account or we would declare bankruptcy, which would stop any foreclosure proceedings indefinitely.

By this time BRT had announced that it was putting 123 West 15th Street up for auction and Lonnie was pushing to include my home condo in the auction. But when it came to the condo, BRT was in third position behind two other lenders with loans totaling $3,000,000. So to see any money BRT would have to auction my condo for what it was worth above $3,000,000, which at the time was nothing. So I didn't think they'd go through with it. But the only way I could stop it for sure would be to declare personal bankruptcy, which I wanted to avoid at all costs. That would have squashed any future credit opportunities for a decade and put an end to any and all hope of turning this ship around.

But it gave us an idea. On September 2, Terrapin Industries filed for bankruptcy. The auction sale of 123 West 15th Street was thus stayed due to the filing. Lonnie didn't auction my condo alone since there was no money to be had there, and we had the collateral account locked up in the courts until we could agree on a settlement in the future with BRT.

So everything was on hold for the moment. We'd won that hand, but it was only a temporary stay of execution.

So I went on looking for financing and made a lot of value engineering changes in the building project to lower the construction cost. This would lessen the funds needed to finance the completion without drastically lowering the sale prices of the condos.

#

Once you file bankruptcy the extreme bottom feeders of the financing world start reaching out their tentacles. They hook you with tempting promises but when you do some digging you usually find out that either the person or the company doesn't even exist. Remember, it's called the World Wide Web for a reason; people from all over the world start coming after you. Why? Because they know you're desperate, starving, hoping that someone out there is real. And you're vulnerable.

In October-November we got an interesting offer. This guy, J. Frankovich of Brandquest said he was interested in buying out Terrapin Industries. This was a no-financing deal. He would pay off BRT with $5,700,000 in cash. Then he would use all my debt to sell the condos virtually tax-free. I would then buy my condo from him. Brandquest was ready to pull the trigger. So was I.

Meanwhile, BRT got our bankruptcy dismissed in regards to 123 West 15th Street. That meant no more stay of execution there. The property was scheduled for auction on November 6.

We were ready to wire BRT the funds on November 5. Then Frankovitch at Brandquest got cold feet. He had some last minute questions on the mechanics' liens and the clear title. So no wire to BRT.

November 6 arrived. Auction day. I went to the court building in Manhattan, where, at 1:30 our green dream went up for auction. It had a retainer of $3,000,000, which meant only bids above $3,000,000 would be accepted. There were maybe seven people in the court and all were looking to bid $1million or less. So no one bid. I spent the whole time talking on the cell to Brandquest and BRT's attorney to get a deal done. No wire, no deal. BRT walked, Frankovitch walked. Back to square one.

#

A fitting end to 2008 came a week before Christmas when the police showed up at my door asking for a search warrant to look for a murdered body on the construction site at 123 West 15th Street. My green dream had now become a probable dump for homicide victims.

Ho, ho, ho.

CHAPTER SEVENTEEN

INTERVENTION

❝ *Do you believe in the devil? You know, a supreme evil being dedicated to the temptation, corruption, and destruction of man?*

Calvin

I'm not sure that man needs the help.

Hobbes

My mother was a strong woman. She was committed to her family and always did everything she could to make sure her children were responsible, caring, and compassionate. She raised us to look out for and help one another.

Mom would jump through flaming hoops for anyone who needed help. Friends, strangers, neighbors. But especially family. I remember she would drive from Connecticut to Montreal, Canada once a month, for years, to take care of her aunt who was over 100 and living by herself. She did that until Aunt Rono died at the age of 107. Why? Because Aunt Rono was family. Mom was that kind of person.

In 2004, Mom had a debilitating stroke.

The saddest part was that it could have been easily averted. A simple dental procedure was her undoing. She was due to have root canal surgery and, like many older Americans, she was on Coumadin to thin her blood. On the advice of her doctor she stopped taking the medication a few days before the procedure because if she started to bleed during the operation it would be hard to stop. Before she had a chance to get back on the drug, she had a stroke.

It was a Friday night and my parents were planning to go to the Stamford

Yacht Club for dinner with friends. They had been doing that for thirty years and my dad still does it today. My father came home from work, as usual, and my mom was getting ready. She was slow getting dressed and wasn't making total sense, slurring her words. But it wasn't really a pronounced thing—could have been just tiredness—and my father didn't think too much of it. So they went to the club as planned. Once they sat down at the table, her speech got noticeably worse and friends began to ask her if she was okay. She said she was fine, but it was becoming obvious by now that something wasn't right.

Finally, an ambulance was called at 8:00 p.m. It came to light afterward that she'd had an aneurism at 3:00 in the afternoon, which had caused the stroke. She'd been coping with it all afternoon as it got progressively worse. As was typical for her, she didn't want to make a fuss and call attention to herself.

The stroke left her paralyzed on the left side of her body. She was wheelchair bound from that point on and needed a full-time nurse to take care of her at home.

She began to spend her days watching television; there wasn't much else she could do. My dad and I got a van with a ramp on the back so we could take her places, mostly to the club to see old friends. Her friends would come by and visit, at least in the beginning. But the visits eventually tapered off. (Her best friend, Mrs. Daly, came by for drinks every Thursday evening until the end. I'll always be grateful to her for that.)

Those were tough times with my mom. She never liked being taken care of; she was always the one who would take care of you. She hated being given a shower or bed bath from the nurse. She would only take a shower if I gave her one and that went on for years. That was heartbreaking and terribly awkward and I don't recommend it to anyone. But it's what you do for family; I'd learned that from mom.

I tried to be there for her as much as possible, but my building project in the city, my family, and my job kept me hopping day and night. No matter how busy I was, though, I made sure I stopped in at least once a week or so, if only for a half hour, just to give Mom updates on the world outside her house. Pam and my girls spent a lot of time with her, too, but not as much as any of us wanted. Never as much as we wanted. I hired a physical therapist for her so she could get some movement going with her body; she was there three days a week until my project imploded. Mom still came to award ceremonies for my sailing trophies and my family spent every holiday with her and my dad. The rest of the siblings were busy with their lives and didn't make it home for visits or the holidays much those years. The holidays were mostly my family and my parents.

That went on for over four years until she had another stroke in June, 2008.

This one put her into a coma. She went into Stamford Hospital on a Friday night. I came out to stay for the weekend and then the following week I went to the hospital every day after work. There wasn't much that could be done. Just try to make her comfortable and hope it ended quickly. It seemed pretty clear that she would not recover from this one. I spent every night with her there; the nurses brought in an extra bed for me. I'd leave every morning at 6:00 to go to work and return at 6:00 every evening. I felt guilty for not having been with her as much as I should have over the previous few years and just hoped she wouldn't suffer.

This was all happening during my whole foreclosure mess. When you're in foreclosure, it's slow death; there are never any quick solutions. Your options just diminish over time, with little hope on the horizon. I was spending literally every free minute trying to get financing in place as the world financial bubble was bursting all around me. My father had lent me substantial money for the project and he was extremely worried about it, which only compounded and exacerbated my problems. I had to give him constant updates on my efforts and respond to cross-examination on an hourly basis. It was a trying time for all of us.

My older brother Tim stopped in that week to see Mom; he lives in Norwalk,

Connecticut. My other two older siblings, Peter and Virginia, flew in the following Friday. Pam and the kids moved up for the weekend from the city and stayed at the yacht club to be nearby. On that Friday afternoon the whole family gathered in her hospital room and stayed with her for a while. I think she had been holding on just to see us all together again and to say goodbye.

I awoke the following morning to a knock on my door. It was my dad.

"She's gone, Colin," was all he said.

Mom's death ripped my father apart. They were married for over fifty years. She'd been his best friend, his confidant, his rock. The funeral was held the following Sunday. All the siblings stayed in town until then. It was the first time all of us had been home and together in over a decade. That was all Mom had ever wanted. It was just too bad she couldn't be there with us.

Before I could even absorb the impact of Mom's passing, the double whammy hit.

My father was worried about my financial problems and the funds he had loaned me. And I think when Mom died he suddenly felt vulnerable in a whole new way. He decided to share the details of his situation with my brothers and sister.

Since growing up, I had never been real close to my siblings. We talked maybe three times a year on the phone, usually on holidays, and that was about it. They'd never made an effort to know me as an adult and, for my part, I really hadn't made much of an effort either. That was the way it was. The most we would do is send presents by mail to each other's kids on the holidays.

They knew I was in financial trouble, but hadn't asked me about it or offered any support. My one attempt to reach out to my brother Tim had been met with a brisk brush-off.

The day after the funeral, I walked into the living room at my parents' house and Tim was sitting there. He looked as if he'd been waiting for me for a while. An awkward sort of heaviness hung in the air.

"We need to talk, Colin," he said in funereal tones. "All of us."

"What's this about?" I asked.

"I think it's better if we wait till everyone's together. We're going to meet in Gaynor's office, tomorrow afternoon."

"Gaynor Brennan? Why?"

"Let's just wait till we're all together."

Gaynor Brennan was the family attorney. Not good. If this was about Mom's will, Tim would have said so. No, this was about something else. Some kind of axe was about to fall. On my neck. "I could feel it coming in the air," as Phil Collins might have said.

So the day of the big meeting arrived. It was me, my brother Tim, my sister Virginia, my dad, my brother Peter on speakerphone (he had to go back to work after the funeral), and Attorney Brennan.

My brother Tim kicked things off and the conversation went something like:

"We've been talking, Colin, and as a family we have some major, major concerns. We know dad's been lending you a lot of money and frankly, it has to stop. We feel you're just using him to finance your lavish lifestyle because you can't admit to yourself that you're financially ruined."

"Whoa," I replied. I'd been expecting hard questions, but not harsh and immediate judgment. "I'm glad you came to this conclusion without even talking to me."

"That's what we're doing right now."

"Is that what this is?" I said. "A talk? Just curious: is anyone interested in hearing my side of this, or would that get in the way of your foregone conclusions?"

Tim gave me the sweeping "you have the floor gesture" and I spent the next thirty minutes describing to them the whole situation with the building, the foreclosure, the lawsuit, and the financing, as well as the courses of actions I and my attorneys were taking to resolve everything.

When I was finished, Tim said, "That's all well and good," as if I hadn't even spoken, "But dad is hemorrhaging money into your project. We just learned that he took out a line of credit on his home in order to keep lending you money. And now, thanks to real estate market, the value of his house has tanked."

"I've been covering his line-of-credit payments," I said, "…at least I was until everything went down the crapper for me."

"Whose fault is it," said Tim, "that everything went down the crapper?"

"This may surprise you," I replied, "but I didn't plan to be defrauded and loose three million dollars and a year's worth of work. I didn't plan to have my insurance company refuse to pay my claim. I didn't plan to have the housing bubble pop in my face. But I'll tell you this: I am going to get this foreclosure settled, I am going to win my lawsuit, and I am going to take care of dad's loan as soon as I get the settlement from the lawsuit."

Attorney Brennan turned to the others at this point. "Just so you know, the steps Colin and his attorneys are taking all seem like good and prudent ones."

"I already gave my ownership in Better Lists back to dad," I reminded them, "so no one can come after the business. I'm doing the best I can here. If anyone has any suggestions as to what I could be doing better, I'd really appreciate hearing them."

But, of course, I knew that wasn't the point of the meeting. The point was to hang me out to dry.

"For starters, you can try admitting to yourself what is obvious to everyone around you," Tim said. "This project of yours is never going to fly. You're borrowing money so you can continue to live your fantasy life of Porsches and nannies. Meanwhile, Dad is on the edge of losing everything."

"Pam and I have a nanny," I replied as calmly as I could, "Because we both work and because it's the most affordable child-care option we could find. I bought my car three years ago and it's more than half paid off and selling it now would be a drop in the bucket compared to what I owe. Plus then I would have to get another car, so it doesn't make sense. I don't know what more I can do."

"I'll tell you exactly what you're going to do," said Tim, and from his tone it was clear that he and the others had already decided. "One, you are going to sell your luxury car. Two, you are going to take a major cut in salary at Better Lists. Three, you are going to move out of your luxury condo in Manhattan and dump it on the market immediately—even if you have to do so at fire sale prices."

"First thing Monday," Virginia chimed in, "I'm taking mom's place as secretary of Better Lists."

"But you've never set foot in the business," I protested. "You've never had the slightest interest in it."

"Regardless, we need someone there to... keep an eye on the family's interests."

"In other words, to watch over me," I said.

"We've arranged so that you have first right of refusal to purchase the building at Better Lists," said Peter over the speaker-phone. He was trying to be conciliatory but I could see what was really going on.

"Well, that's very generous," I said, "seeing as how you all know I'm in no position to be buying a building." The real motive behind that move was to allow them to sell the building out from under Better Lists Inc. should my father die. Which was fine, really. Better Lists would probably be better off renting its facilities. I could understand that. What I couldn't understand was the adversarial nature of their attack, the deliberate hurtfulness and judgment. Why were they adding to my problems rather than offering a listening ear? Wasn't family supposed to come together when one of them was in trouble? Why were they coming after me like bloodthirsty creditors and foreclosure attorneys? Why were they trying to restrict my only income from a business that I had been working at for thirty years, at a time when I desperately needed money?

Was this what our mother would have wanted? Had they waited till she died to turn on me because they knew she never would have stood for it when she was alive?

The answer to all of these questions became clear when Tim looked me in the eye and said in a low voice, presumably so that dad couldn't hear, "I'm not going to take care of him financially just because you lost all your money."

I looked to Virginia for support and she shot me a look that said, "me either."

Ah, so there it was. They weren't concerned about my financial problems, they were worried about potential problems for them. They were worried about my father's financial situation because it might affect their situation if they had to help my father out in retirement. That was the crux of the matter. I was a financial dead man in their eyes and they wanted to limit the fallout on them.

I get that sometimes you need to make tough decisions in a family. I get that if you're dealing with a family member who's a thief or an addict, for instance, and you've tried your hardest to solve the problem in other ways, you sometimes need to draw a line in the sand. But they'd never offered me any kind of help or support. Now it was clear. I was just a business liability. We'd bypassed the whole "brother" thing. This "intervention" wasn't about me, it was about them. They were out for blood. There was nothing more to be said.

I had enough problems; I couldn't take my siblings turning on me too. I got up and walked out. I have not talked to my brother, Tim or my sister, Virginia since that day.

I was destroyed by this, to say the least. Not just for myself but for my mother's memory. I had been brought up with the idea that you take care of your family. I had always supported my parents and they had always supported me. We were there for each other; I guess my siblings missed that memo. I wasn't looking for help or money from them; just a little understanding and flexibility.

After the meeting my father felt terrible. It had not been his intention to put me on the hot seat. He just felt scared after my mother died and wanted his other children to understand what was happening with him, money-wise. Ultimately he knew I supported him and would continue to do so, as I had for the past thirty years, running the business alongside him.

My siblings went home again and the drama cleared. Dad and I went back to work. Had I done as my brother Tim had told me that day my family would have been on the streets and Better Lists Inc. would have ceased to exist.

Thankfully, I didn't. I continued on and very slowly things began to turn around. I got $130,000 of the TD Waterhouse Collateralized account returned to my dad, and Better Lists kept on chugging along. I paid back my brother Tim some money he had recently loaned my father (under the condition that Dad take a series of steps against me). My father realized, I think, that his other children would not help him in the long run. It was not in their nature. Dad and I came to the conclusion that we were in the same boat and that it was up to us to continue working together as Mom had always wanted.

I promised him I would get us both out of this mess. It would take time, but I *would* get us out of this mess.

CHAPTER EIGHTEEN

SETTLEMENTS

❝❞*I'm interested in anything about revolt,
disorder, chaos, especially activity that
appears to have no meaning. It seems to me
to be the road toward freedom.*

Jim Morrison

Pam and I used to joke to each other, "When did you first discover they were out to get you?" Once the debts started piling up and the foreclosure mess started, we had to shift into Witness Protection gear in our personal lives. I couldn't have a bank account in my name anymore; any funds I had were kept in business accounts so no one could attach them. I had to screen all calls at work and refer collection agents only to my cell phone, which I never, NEVER answered unless I knew who was calling. I have folders upon folders of correspondence on all my debts; if you saw the stacks you'd think I worked for the DOB.

We continued to look for financing in the beginning of 2009, even though a personal reference letter from God wouldn't have been enough. I procured a few more useless letters of intent for mortgages and had beaucoup meetings with financiers, including a couple of Swiss bankers who looked like they stepped out of a cartoon. This cost us another borrowed $35,000 for letters of intent. These, of course, resulted in approximately $0 net funds for us, with the supposed lenders disappearing and turning off their phones. I was desperately hoping that someone out there was real and could provide us actual, non-Monopoly money, but the credit stream was bone dry. What chance did I have to get financing if GE Capital couldn't even get overnight loans on the cash exchange?

Pam and I became wanted people. We'd defaulted on the mortgage on our condo with Countrywide as of November of '07 and were foreclosed upon on

March 11, 2008 after the account was taken over by Bank of America. So we were living in fear of being kicked out on the streets (and without our lawyers Andy Albstein, Matthew Hearle, Christopher Clark and Kevin Nash at GWU, that's what would have happened.)

That fear went on for six years, three months and five days.

As I mentioned before, our Chapter 11 petition for bankruptcy for Terrapin Industries LLC was dismissed in January, 2009 after BRT objected to it. (They didn't want us to declare bankruptcy because then we wouldn't have had to pay them and the property would be held until all debts were settled.) When that fell apart, our last hope for reorganizing the project under some kind of protective structure evaporated. That's when the dam broke.

Promises and small payments could no longer hold off the contractors. They all slapped liens on 123 West 15th Street—Garadice for $177,450, Speedway Plumbing for $20,000, Superior Concrete for $59,681 (I resolved this one by signing over our $150,000 car lift to them that they were storing for me already), Norfast Consulting for $4,022, Gilsanz Murray for $16,951.

The liens put the last nail in the financing coffin; no one would finance a property with multiple liens on it, especially during a severe credit crunch.

It was official, our green dream was dead. I had tried my best and put everything I had into this project, but economic times had changed, probably forever. With the collapse of the finance market, America's two-tiered society had become even more polarized; the haves and the have-nots had taken a giant step further apart. Everyday people will never see credit like that again.

So be it. Thy will be done.

It was time to get the best arrangement possible and walk away from 123 West 15th Street with a few remnants of my tattered shirt still clinging to my back.

BRT finally realized I was finished. As of February, 2009, I had lost over $13,000,000 and was in a truly comical amount of debt. Up till then, the good folks at BRT had thought I might have some more money they could squeeze out of me, but now they knew I was wrung out. They realized they needed to salvage the property before it was too late. Other projects at BRT had gone bad; they had some larger condo projects in Florida that went belly up. So they were feeling the crunch. They were finally ready to negotiate a deal. One that I hoped would not require blood sacrifices of my children.

First step with BRT was settling the foreclosure of 123 West 15th Street. Next step was the release of my condo from BRT's foreclosure. Finally, we had to resolve the issue of the excess funds in the TD Waterhouse Collateral Loan account. This was not going to be quick and easy.

A sailing friend of mine, Bugs Baer, likes to say, "Wealth may not last, but debt is forever." I planned on making forever as short as possible.

All I wanted now was the ability to walk away from 123. BRT made an offer. Their settlement stipulated that I would get my life policies back and the BRT lien on my condo at 121 West 15th Street would be released one year from February 19, 2009 provided I helped the new owner of 123 with his project documentation and didn't obstruct his construction for one year. BRT would also release claims on the excess funds in the collateral account at TD Bank.

In return BRT would get $20,000 as a settlement fee. BRT would also get 50% from my lawsuit against PL&S, or $300,000, whichever was greater. That lawsuit was estimated to come in at $2-$5 million at the time. BRT would, of course, get the building at 123 West 15th Street too, along with all the plans, files, documents, and permits to finish the development, and also my help to finish the project and to try to get back any funds back from my contractors' deposits.

In short, they wanted my building and my help to finish it within a year. Fair enough, really.

Basically I became BRT's indentured servant for fourteen months. In reality it didn't go too badly. BRT gave up on collecting anything from my contractors shortly after closing and I just had to get a lot of stuff notarized and walk the new owners through any problems they were having with the DOB.

So six and half years after I started it, the project that had been my passion and my obsession was cast off the rocks for the last time. It was time to abandon ship, get in the lifeboat, and paddle towards shore.

We had fought a good fight and had lost a lot along the way. I owed my father millions from all of his help on the project over a six-year period, on top of all my other debts. He'd believed in me and had done more to help than I'd had any right to ask. His is a debt that I will never be able to fully repay and it eats at me every day of my life. I do my best to make Better Lists profitable and his life as good as I can. As of September 2014, I will have been working with him for 30 years. It's what I can do for now.

BRT was very anxious to sell 123 West 15th Street before the market fell any further. And the bottom, at that time, appeared to be nowhere in sight. So the property at 123 West 15th Street went back on the market on February 20, 2009, the day after BRT and I made our agreements. Asking price: $5,250,000. Massey Knakal, the realtor, put it up for sale, along with a rendering of what they proposed the finished building could look like—a square pillbox with balconies right out of the third Reich. It was so gosh darn aesthetically appealing that a month later the price dropped to $4,875,000, It finally sold for $2,800,000 on June 24. Wow. BRT would have gotten a lot more if they had worked with me earlier. Nice job, Lonnie.

BRT had to finance the deal with a guy named Ken Hart of Helco Construction on a one-year note at BRT's usual hard money interest rate (13.5%). This, of course, came with a drop-dead completion date or the ownership would revert back to BRT. The typical strong-arm crap BRT was known for. Before Hart got started on the project I needed to finish 121 West 15th Street's sidewalk and building front, and anything else I could get done, while I still had the permits. Because once construction on 123 West 15th Street got started (again) I would not be able to finish 121 until 123 was complete.

We added a nice wave-formation brick sidewalk to 121 that had radiant heat to melt snow, a New Orleans cast iron fence, and gates to the street. The sidewalk barricade was removed for the first time since 2006. At last 121 was completely finished, with no more scaffolds! It felt good to make actual, observable progress on a building for the first time in years. Phase one of our dream project was finally finished, as of June 29, 2009.

123 West 15th Street went into construction under its new ownership. The first thing they did was tear down all the steel I had put up—the steel that

had cost me a king's ransom and that had come to represent all my hopes and dreams for the project. It was cut into pieces and sold for scrap. Ken Hart was doing a more modest commercial design and would not be needing structural steel as substantial as the stuff I'd installed.

Hart built a basic six-story, stone-facade building. Strictly vanilla, no character at all. He kept the sidewalk curb cut and garage, though. Interestingly enough, he also built in the structural capacity to add a cantilevered penthouse later using the partition wall between the buildings. And in February of 2014, in what is perhaps this story's most ironic twist, I sold 121's roof rights to the 3rd floor condo owner and made a deal with the new owner of 123 so that the cantilevered penthouse we originally envisioned could at last be built. So eleven years after we started all this, our bold design will finally become a reality, it just won't be ours. But at least it will make Boddington roll over in his "final parking spot." Hey, that's something. It's the little things in life.

The new building at 123, someone said, looks like a funeral home on steroids. But beauty is in the eye of the beholder, right? Truth was, it no longer mattered to me what it looked like. It could have been a six-story Taco Bell for all I cared. I was done with 123 West 15th Street. Finis. It was time to move on and get my life back together. A little rebirth was in order.

We decided to lease a sailboat that summer to get away from our troubles and see if our big world-sailing dream still had legs. We leased a Hanse 470 from Sound Waters Sailing Center in Norwalk, CT, and went on the New York Yacht Club Cruise with the kids—sailing, swimming, and just having fun. It was good to be back on the water again. It had been too long since I'd captained a boat and the kids loved it. Something about sailing that gives you a renewed outlook on life.

We got away for a couple more sailing weekends that summer, and soon we could feel our master plan itching to be reborn. The original idea had been to build a green building that we could sell as condos and make money to sail around the world. Okay, so fate had thrown a bit of a monkey wrench into the works, but that didn't mean the end goal had to be abandoned. We just needed to rework the plan.

First step was to figure out what kind of boat we should do our travels in. It had to hold our family of five, and our dog and cats, and be seaworthy. So leasing the 470 was a step in the right direction. It's always a good idea to try out a boat on a week-long trip before purchasing one.

You may be wondering where I was going to get money to buy a boat. Patience, patience. All in good time. Keep in mind I never stopped working full-time through this whole drama so there was always income rolling in. I never stopped scheming for the dream either. Now that our expenses were finally decreasing dramatically, an alternate plan was starting to take shape. But we still had a few more issues to resolve...

#

BRT tried to delay the return of my condo to me and didn't actually release their lien on it until March 12, 2010, a month later than contractually agreed. They did this only after I pressured them by refusing to help any further with 123 West 15th Street. BRT's attorney also didn't want to release the lien until the TD Waterhouse lawsuit was settled. But I knew that Ken Hart, the new owner of 123, wanted to get his Certificate of Occupancy, and I had the power to hold it up if BRT didn't honor its end of the contract. After several weeks of heated emails, they gave me a release on the condo, but not a complete release on me personally. The devil will never withdraw his talons if not compelled to.

BRT's release of the condo lien was only one part of our condo problem. Remember, the condo was still under foreclosure with lenders one and two, Bank of New York (Bank of America, originally through Countrywide), and National Bank. They were the ones that held the big mortgages.

We finally got BRT to give us back the excess funds in the Collateral Holding Account at TD Waterhouse (TD Bank) as agreed to in the settlement, but there was still a pending suit we'd initiated against TD Waterhouse. Remember, these were excess funds we'd placed in the collateral account at TD Waterhouse to cover any margin calls on the account due to stock fluctuations. These funds were specifically not part of the collateral we had put up for BRT. But we had to sue TD Waterhouse to stop BRT from liquidating these funds (most of them were in stocks). So once we settled with BRT on 123 West 15th Street and BRT released any hold on the uncollateralized funds, my father finally got that $130,000 back. Which was a good thing. But, of course, in the litigious world we live in, it never ends there.

TD Bank wanted compensation for their legal fees in defending our lawsuit against them for illegally releasing the excess funds to BRT. I had all the agreements with TD Bank, signed by several officers, stating over and over again, in black-and-white, that the excess funds in the account were not collateralized. But still I had to sue TD Bank to stop them from releasing these funds to BRT. Now they wanted us to pay their legal fees! As Russian comic

Yakov Smirnoff used to say, "America: What a country!" TD Waterhouse actually sent out a letter stating they were going to automatically remove the funds for their legal expenses from our account. We were not okay with this. My dad emptied the account that day.

We counter-motioned against TD for holding our funds as the stock market crashed, which caused a tremendous loss in value. As with most suits, it was finally resolved in negotiation. You would not believe the meetings we had on this one, not to mention the multiple court appearances. Hours of both sides stating the same thing over and over at a table full of lawyers making $450 an hour. In the end BRT paid TD Bank $50,000 and we paid $10,000 for the lawsuit settlement. It galled me to pay anything, but at this point I just wanted to finish this thing and walk away.

Okay, so two of our four big issues were settled. We were getting closer to freedom. Or some version of it.

The third issue was our lawsuit against PL&S and the others. This was our ace in the hole. This was going to be our big payday; the suit that was going to turn us around financially. We would finally get justice from those dirt-bag insurance companies. We had already poured over $200,000 in legal fees into this lawsuit (in NY State you cannot sue to recover legal fees, by the way; you can guess who made up that rule) and it was time for them to pay. Again, the expected compensation from the lawsuit was between $2,000,000 and $5,000,000.

September 7th 2009, Scottsdale Insurance (PL&S's insurance company) presented a motion to remove them from the lawsuit because they had not been notified correctly about it. (Richie Donato disappeared and we notified Scottsdale directly and correctly, but of course insurance lawyers try every angle to worm out of paying.) We fought against it, but the judge agreed with them and in 2010 released Scottsdale from the suit. In theory this should not have been a huge deal because we already had a judgment against PL&S for $860,000 and the total policy was for only $1,000,000. But it was a big deal because that $860K judgment was against Richie personally and PL&S. Meaning: that and a subway token would get you a ride on the subway. All we had to do was find Richie's assets, seize them, and liquidate them. Good luck with that. We couldn't find his ass, never mind his assets.

Still, though, the bigger suits were the ones against Certified Testing Labs for falsifying reports and the Hartford for failure to honor its builders risk claim. These still represented millions.

Three-plus years after we sued all of them—remember, these guys in the insurance industry have bottomless pockets and just try to outlast you— our attorney Kevin Nash finally suggested that we go to mediation. We had finished discovery and were setting up a court date to go to trial, but that would cost us more money, and we were running on empty.

So we went to mediation with high hopes that justice would prevail over premeditated fraud and collusion amongst insurance companies.

The way mediation works is that an impartial attorney or retired judge guides a negotiated settlement of the case. This referee is paid per case, per day, at a pretty hefty rate, but in this case that fee was nominal considering the alternative. "Impartial" was the problem, though. These paid arbitrators are usually insurance lawyers or big-law-firm attorneys that have at one time or another sat on the side of the table representing an insurance company against a "nobody" like us. Bonds in the Old Boys' network run deep, and impartiality in the legal profession is an oxymoron. We knew that going in, but we were hopeful that Justice, if she could not remain completely blind, would at least wear an eye-patch over one eye.

Ah, Grasshopper, you still have much to learn.

On May 4th, 2010 we had our first of two mediations at Robinson & Cole LLP on the 28th floor of the large oval building at 885 Third Avenue. We had the two conference rooms on either end of the oval. Great views of midtown, but I was not exactly in the mood to admire the views.

I came with my attorneys Kevin Nash and Christopher Clark. The Hartford showed up with four attorneys. Certified Testing Labs brought two attorneys and smiling Richard Zaloum. And, of course, there was the ref. All eleven of us sat down at a big conference table and all of us were on the clock except Zaloum and myself.

We exchanged pleasantries, established the ground rules, presented our positions, and then split off into separate rooms. Then, all day long, the referee would pop in and out of both rooms. Fielding offers and counter offers, with a little drama tossed in as we rejected ridiculous bids.

I had hired an independent insurance expert (an attorney) prior to the mediation to review the case to give me the extra edge I felt I would need. So we had our case down pat and held a strong position. The next seven hours, from 10 a.m. to 5 p.m., we played the Shuttle Negotiation Game, breaking only for lunch, which was delivered.

At the close of the day, they made us the mind-bogglingly inadequate offer of $500,000. We walked away from the table. The referee urged us all to meet again. It took three weeks to coordinate all eleven schedules and get us back in the same room.

The second mediation happened on May 24. I walked in the door determined to not take less than $2,400,000. We made it clear at the start of the day that we needed to be talking in the millions, not the thousands.

CTL's attorney responded by saying something like, "In the interest of cutting to the chase, you should know that we only have $625,000, absolute maximum, remaining for settlement of the policy. The policy was only valued at $1,000,000 and we have already used $375,000 on legal fees. So six-twenty-five is our maximum operating range. And, for reasons we choose not to get into here, we do not intend to pay the maximum."

Then Hartford's lawyer added: "We have decided to put a hard deadline on settlement. If this isn't resolved today, we're going to restart the discovery process. That will likely delay trial for another two years."

 On top of that, Kevin Nash, my own attorney, took me aside and reminded me, "If this goes forward, I cannot work on contingency. We have to resolve this today or you're going to need to be prepared to find other legal counsel that will do a contingency deal. Oh, and don't forget—BRT still has to be negotiated with." Remember, BRT was contractually due to get $300,000 or 50% of the suit settlement, whichever was higher. That alone, after fees and other payments, would pretty much wipe out any settlement of less than a couple million. It also effectively killed the hope of doing any kind of future contingency deal with another lawyer.

By late morning, Nash saw the writing on the wall and suggested we lower our asking price considerably. He knew the game and how to win it. In his blue pinstripe suit, rough beard, he constantly presented the facts of fraud. Only to be rebutted by legal BS from the Insurance company counsel that had nothing to debunk the fraud. But, the fact was there was only so much money on the table.

Fuck.

Another lunch was brought into the conference room, but I couldn't eat. I was shaking all over. My boat was sinking again. What was I going to do? This lawsuit had represented my only hope, my only way to get back on my feet, but with the reduced numbers we were talking today, I'd be walking away with nothing. I, my family, my father, and my future would be screwed.

I'd spent a fortune pressing this lawsuit and believed I was a hundred percent in the right. From the day I started my building project I had played by the rules, done everything legally and ethically, abided by all the DOB regulations, and eaten a truckload of shit, only to be screwed every inch of the way by people who did the complete opposite. Contractors, insurance companies, tenants, neighbors, the DOB—they all openly lied and cheated. Aided and abetted by lawyers, of course, who ran up billable hours into six- or seven-figure tabs or took a third of everything.

And now my last hope for justice was circling the drain.

That was when it hit me, full on and undiluted: America really had turned into a very dark place, a place where corruption and deceit ruled the day. Justice was for sale to whoever had the fattest checkbook. Truth and hard work literally mattered nothing at all. I had played by the rules and gotten screwed by doing it. Screwed to the bone. I literally felt sick to my stomach. This was not the country I had grown up in—or thought I'd grown up in. And this was not a country I wanted to raise my children in. Period. End of discussion.

I resolved in that moment, with a one-hundred-percent, take-no-prisoners attitude, that I and my family would find a way to get back on a sailboat, as soon as we possibly could, and we would leave this place. And never come back.

It was time to get out of the US of A and return to the only place that made any sense to me. The sea.

SYL, assholes.

Negotiations hadn't improved much by late afternoon. I lost it.

"I'm out of here," I said to my lawyer Kevin Nash, slapping my hands on the marble-topped conference table. "Get the best deal you can and I'll look at it in the morning." I needed a drink. I stormed out the door to get one.

The deal Kevin got us was for $900,000. He negotiated BRT down to accepting $275,000. He took $350,000, my father got $206,000 and BRT made us put $10,000 into escrow for TD Waterhouse suit. I took the remaining $59,000 and what did I do with it?

Leased a racing sailboat, High Noon, and did the Newport Bermuda Race and got a 5th in my division. My family met me in Bermuda for a nice vacation.

Was this the most responsible thing I could do with the money?

Responsible? I literally didn't know what the word meant anymore. I thought I'd been acting responsibly for the past decade. And where had it gotten me? The most responsible thing I could do right now was get my family out of here.

The insurance company took another three weeks to actually fund the settlement. I found out when I arrived in port in Bermuda that the funds had finally been wired. When I got my hands on that money I resolved that I would never, ever wait for lawyers again. For over a decade I had put my life on hold, waiting for legal decisions, wires, funding... Waiting for other people to decide my fate. Life is too short. It was time for me to seize the ship's wheel of my own life.

All I needed was a way.

CHAPTER NINETEEN

PERSEVERE

> **❝** *On a planet that increasingly resembles one huge Maximum Security prison, the only intelligent choice is to plan a jail break.*
>
> *Robert Anton Wilson*

A few years ago a friend of Pam's gave us a plaque cut out of rustic decorative steel. It was one word: "Persevere." The gift was to remind us that there was light at the end of the tunnel and to help us fight through all the drama that had been consuming our lives for so long. This friend had been going through some real estate troubles similar to ours on a development in Florida and thought the plaque would help us. I put it on the wall of my home office and looked at it every time I sat at my desk.

It was just a word, but the plaque came to symbolize hope for my family during those six years of foreclosure. We all knew deep down that we would get through this. Somehow. There was no quick fix, but if we stayed the course and kept on doing our best every day, our troubles would eventually end and we'd be able to start over. It was never a question of if, but when. The plaque was a daily reminder of that.

The family—all of the children were involved—decided that Persevere would be the name of the boat we were going to sail around the world in. Whenever we were finally able to buy it. Pam and I thought the name was perfect. Of course, we still needed to figure out a way to buy that boat, but somehow looking at its name on our wall every day helped to visualize it.

So the word became not just a symbol of encouragement, but a promise of freedom on the open seas.

We even learned that the Chinese symbol for "persevere" comes from an old Chinese proverb involving koi. This really resonated with us because we had been living with koi in the mini-Yangtze River in our living room since 2001. Koi were our daily companions, swimming under our feet as we carried a cup of tea across the room.

How did koi come to symbolize perseverance? According to Kenneth Koi on his website *Koi Story*...

An ancient tale tells of a huge school of golden koi swimming upstream the Yellow River in China. ...When they reached a waterfall at the end of the river, many of the koi turned back, letting the flow of the river carry them away. The remaining koi refused to give up. Leaping from the depths of the river, they attempted to reach the top of the waterfall to no avail. Their efforts caught the attention of local demons, who mocked their efforts and heightened the waterfall out of malice. After a hundred years of jumping, one koi finally reached the top of the waterfall. The gods recognized the koi for its perseverance and determination and turned it into a golden dragon, the image of power and strength.

The golden dragon symbol, we decided, would adorn all of the crew shirts and the racing battle flag of the boat.

The sea, the sea, it called us onward...

#

The first year under foreclosure you're always worried you're going to be thrown out on the street. Then you meet with your attorney and he assures you this is a long process and, worst-case scenario, it will take two-plus years for them to get your ass out the door. And that's if everything goes against you; usually it takes even longer. Knowing this, you slowly start to put it in the back of your mind. Every once in a while you get a new summons and a fresh wave of panic hits you. But you get used to it.

It's strange what we humans get used to. Give us a little time and we adapt to anything. Concentration camps. Martial law. Bill O'Reilly.

When you're under foreclosure, low-level anxiety becomes your new norm. You begin to realize—at least I did—that there is no security out there anymore, so what's a little more insecurity going to hurt you? I understand our situation was a bit extreme, but there are a couple million people out there living under foreclosure and another ten million living underwater (with a mortgage larger than the value of their home). Job security is gone now. No one has a "stable career" with a company anymore—a pension plan and a gold watch at retirement. Only if you work for the government and that's going to get phased out sooner or later. If you think your job is stable, you're probably just deluding yourself. It could be gone tomorrow if your company decides to outsource or a new technology puts you out of business. Medical security doesn't exist. If you're lucky enough to have health insurance, your plan may be changed on you without warning, and your premium might suddenly shoot through the roof. Anytime you set foot in a hospital, you might contract something horrible or have a surprise bill show up for hundreds or thousands of dollars. It seems like everything we eat and do gives us cancer or is actually unhealthy, and 9/11 propaganda blew up the comfy notion that we were safe from enemy attack on our own soil (from within or without).

Security is an illusion. So learn to live with insecurity. That was the lesson. Not just for us but for everyone living under the new normal.

Once we settled the lawsuit and got out from under BRT's thumb in 2010, we'd had enough of the city and decided we needed a change of scenery. We rented out our condo and moved into a rented house in Tokeneke, a seaside neighborhood on the edge of Darien, Connecticut. The plan was to decompress for a while, plan for our getaway, and save some money too. The condo in Chelsea fetched us $10,000 a month (2300 square feet, 3 bedrooms, 2 baths, 3 fireplaces duplex) while the house in Tokeneke cost us $3500 a month (2000 square feet, 3 bedrooms, 2 baths, and 1 fireplace). A $6500-a-month difference. We could put some of it toward a boat! Meanwhile, the kids could get a taste of life in the burbs. Up till then they'd only known city life.

We decided on Tokeneke because it was close to my office and they had just built a $50,000,000 elementary school for just 400 kids. Plus the place was full of empty homes for rent. Land is the big-ticket item in Tokeneke. It's highly coveted and there isn't any more of it available. So a lot of people bought small houses in order to acquire the land, with the plan of building larger houses and selling them. But the financial crisis left a lot of them stranded and unable to build due to lack of funds. So now they had these "small" houses that they would rather rent out at bargain rates than leave empty.

The kids toured the school and loved it. The house we rented was within walking distance, so they walked to school every day. The dog had a yard to romp in. The kids played in the pond next door, went sailing, we did burb-y things. I still managed the condo association for our building in Chelsea and did maintenance. I was in the city once or twice a week for business anyway, so stopping by the condo wasn't a problem.

We were Bridge and Tunnel people now. Life was okay—well, livable. Life in the burbs is a trip of its own.

I still had a few major problems to resolve. First and foremost was the foreclosure on the condo from Bank of New York (Bank of America) for $2,720,000 and the second one from National Bank for $257,000. We had been in foreclosure since March 11, 2008. I had taken out these two mortgages to pay off BRT so I could get a second round of funding from them after the accident at the work site. All of the money went directly to BRT to pay down my mortgage with them. American Express also had a personal judgment against me for $251,000 for the Terrapin Industries LLC business charge account that I used for paying contractors.

So I still had these major debts but it was slowly getting better. I was down to three major debts from a total of 32 in 2007. Not too bad. It was progress. Slow, steady progress. Persevere, persevere.

I knew I would never have good credit again (yet another reason to sail off into the sunset), but I did want to pay my debts. I'd had a settlement offer from National Bank back in 2007 for $25,000. I didn't have the money to pay them then. They'd written off the debt already. I thought they would probably take the same deal again when I finally got my hands on some cash. American Express offered to settle for $50,000 and give me back the credit card. They wrote that one off in 2008 and I figured they, too, would take the same deal down the road when I could afford it. Turned out, National stuck to their guns and would not negotiate at all while the house was still inhabited and they had a second lien on the property. So I would have to settle with them whenever I finally sold my condo (assuming I could pull that off).

Bottom line: there was no pressing reason to settle with National or American Express until I resolved the first mortgage. My main priority at this point was to find a way to get my family onto a boat. There was no longer any doubt in our minds that this was the right course of action. Though it may sound outrageously extravagant to be even considering buying a boat, given the financial shape I was in, to me it was the only thing that made any sense at all. The boat was going to be my family's sole home and vehicle for the foreseeable future, as well as a way to begin achieving victory in my life again.

I met with Martin Van Breems at Sound Waters Sailing in Norwalk and started talking about purchasing a Hanse 545 for the 2011 NYYC (New York Yacht Club), RORC (Royal Offshore Racing Club) Transatlantic Race. Oddly enough, it's cheaper to buy a boat for a transatlantic race than to lease one, and I had a few friends at New York Yacht Club who were interested in going in on one together. So I did it—I made a down payment on the Hanse 545 and Pam and I flew to Dusseldorf in January 2011 to finalize the sale.

That trip to Germany was the first time Pam and I had been away together, without the children, since the twins were born in 2005. We love our kids, but Pam and I needed this. So we decided to take a five-day detour to Amsterdam. A full week of adult conservation and dining out was like heaven. We hadn't traveled abroad in years. It felt amazingly good to be alive again, focused on the future and on positive possibilities rather than on liabilities, fears, and regrets. It really was a transformative week.

We liked the Hanse yacht because of its modern design and open interior, plus the fact that the boat was quick; she could cruise easily at 8-10 knots. One of the big pluses was that she could be sailed single-handedly but also raced competitively with a full crew. All of the halyards & sheets came back to the cockpit and it had an electric winch and a good autopilot. So when I was with my family I could sail her solo without killing myself by running all over the boat. She could also be raced competitively against Swan 42s and several other boats in her class. And win.

We had her designed to our specifications. We had the keel extended to facilitate ocean crossing and racing performance. This would make the draft 9½ feet and allow her to hold more sail. I changed the back stays to running back stays (these add mast support and are good for open-ocean racing), installed a Seldén carbon rig with hydraulic jack for mast tuning, and ordered a full set of North sails to increase racing performance. Pam picked out the interior touches and galley appliances with the dealer.

Crazy to be buying a boat? Yes. Totally insane? Definitely. Would not have it any other way.

The boat arrived in May, 2011. It was too late for the 2011 transatlantic race (but we are already signed & paid up for the 2015 transatlantic race!). It would not have been smart to do a shakedown race (a "test" race you do with a new racing craft to expose any possible structural or equipment problems) across the Atlantic with a boat only three weeks old. You'd be in the middle of the Atlantic if anything went wrong. I focused instead on getting her ready for the future. We took the next three years to fully equip Persevere, make her seaworthy for our global adventure, race her locally, and get the family prepared for living and schooling aboard her.

One cool—and, yes, extravagant—thing we did was to have the hull wrapped with an image from one of the artists we got to know when we ran the gallery in the city. A boat wrap is just like the ones you see on cars and trucks on the street (basically a large, self-adhesive photograph made of plastic), except on a boat it also protects the hull. The image we chose was a section of our oil painting by Javier Lopez Barbosa. He is an emotional, bright-hue, abstract painter. Mac Designs out of Newport, Rhode Island (who wraps all the Volvo

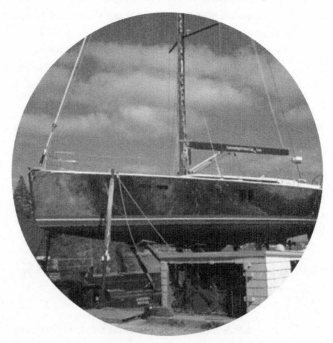

Race Sail Boats) did the wrap for Persevere. Duggal Graphics in Manhattan took two weeks to scan in a five by ten inch section of the original painting. It took that long to remove any pixels from the graphics at blown-up scale. It came out great. Persevere would be photographed everywhere she went from then on, showing off her abstract hull colors of blue, green, purple, and red.

She remained in dry dock throughout 2011 as we updated all our American and Canadian passports (I have dual citizenship and so do all my children). 2011 was a work and learn-about-the-Persevere year. I also introduced a new sailing product to the world that year and did several sailboat trade shows. The product was the Sailors Night Vision Cap (www.SailorsNightVisipnCap. com). It's a baseball cap with red and white LED lights built into it to allow sailors to see better at night hands free. Pam did the trade shows with me and attended a lot of seminars about long-term cruising and live-aboard boating. So that was good education for Pam and the kids and good exposure for my product. We sold over 7000 caps the first few years and they are still selling strong.

The next year, 2012, I paid off the carbon mast and had it installed. Persevere was finally launched. We registered her in Rhode Island, mainly because that state does not require sales tax on maritime purchases. We docked her in Jamestown, just across the bay from Newport. We mostly just cruised that first year; I didn't have my racing sails yet. I still needed funds to pay for those. We got Aspen, our dog, acclimated to the boat and he proved an able seaman. He would do his business on the bow and I would wash it off with a deck-wash hose. He took to swimming too. We were lucky there; some Malamutes love the water, others hate it. We started a series of steps to make sure that the cruising life would work for my family over the next couple years.

We did the New York Yacht Club Cruise around southern New England for seven days. It gave the family a chance to see what it would be like living on the boat with the dog and traveling. The kids attended sailing school every summer to get their sea legs. They got a lot of small boat sailing experience and Breana actually started racing little Opti boats. She was chosen Most

Improved Sailor at Noroton Yacht Club in 2012. The girls were swimming and sailing every day. The whole family, including the pets, seemed to take to the nautical life, which was a great relief. I don't know what we'd have done if one of us turned out to be a serious landlubber.

Persevere wintered at Jamestown Boat Yard that year and got updated with full B&G Zeus instruments, a chart plotter, Iridium Satellite phone, radar, autopilot, towed generator, two life rafts for 14 people, and all the safety equipment, EPIRBS (Emergency Position Indicating Radio Beacons) and PLBs (Personal Locator Beacons) required for Category 1 offshore racing.

We docked Persevere in Newport the summer of 2013. It was a big year for her. We logged over 3000 miles, racing and cruising that summer. It was a good break-in period with very few major problems. The family lived aboard the boat full time, as prep for the Big Trip, and the kids went to sailing school at Sail Newport. I drove up every Friday and back every Monday at 4 a.m. to go to work. The kids loved on-boat living. We all did. Persevere was beginning to feel like home to us. Which was the whole point. The idea was to spend as much time as possible aboard her with the family. I have heard horror stories of families attempting to do a circumnavigation without much preparation. Disaster is usually the result. Not that they all get hurt or killed, usually they divorce. Close quarters for long periods of time can really test a family.

I finally got to campaign (race) Persevere that summer of 2013. This was important because it put her through the paces and let me learn her strengths and limits. You don't want any unpleasant surprises when you're in the middle of a major race or out in the middle of the Atlantic with your family in a storm. My crew jumped at a chance to race aboard her and we put her through some rough seas that summer.

Persevere's first regatta was the Block Island Race in May (Memorial Day weekend, my birthday). We took second place in our division. Not bad for a first race. We had a Swan 42 follow us for hours down Long Island Sound, unable to pass. Persevere was too quick. She likes strong winds since she is a heavy boat. The family had fun and it was good to pick up some silver again.

We scheduled four races that summer.

The start of the Annapolis-Newport Race was delayed by a hurricane. It was a wet race and the wind died along the way from the vacuum of the storm. Persevere took fifth in our division—respectable, but nothing to uncork the Dom about. It was nice to see she could sail through heavy seas, though. Then Edgartown Yacht Club 'Round-the-Island race was a beautiful run around Martha's Vineyard. The twins joined the crew and they loved it. We had a lot of fun and spent a few days on the island. At the end of the summer came the Vineyard Race. During that one we got a major line wrap that my foredeck guy couldn't clear from the rig. We lost four hours dealing with that. Persevere received a fifth place in our division, out of the money. All in all, the first racing season turned out pretty well with no major problems.

We also did the NYYC cruise in 2013, which went up to Maine that year. An old childhood friend of mine and his family came with my family and we had a blast. Maine's coast is astonishingly beautiful.

The family really got their sea legs that fall with the Salty Dawg Rally from Annapolis, Virginia to West End, Tortola. A total of 1300 miles. We took the whole gang this time, complete with Aspen the dog and our two cats Wasabi and Ginger. We left on a Thursday morning with a breezy 10-20 knot reach. The afternoon sail was pleasant and I fished off the back of the boat for the first time. Within an hour I caught a nice fifteen-pound tuna. We immediately cut it up and had sashimi with soy sauce. A nice way to start our trip, but I knew the weather was going to be rough crossing the Gulf Stream.

By dusk the seas built up to seven feet and the wind grew to 30 knots. The whole family was seasick, passing the bucket around and sleeping on deck under the bimini (canvas top) in the cockpit. The weather was too rough for autopilot. I stayed at the helm for two days, around the clock.

Dawn broke on day two and it was still rough. I called in on the satellite phone to confirm the updates to the weather forecasts from the Salty Dawg Rally weather advisor. I was told that we should expect 50-knot winds that night, but after that we'd be past our troubles and there would be a 15-knot reach the rest of the way to Tortola.

I spent the rest of the day changing jib sails to storm jibs and preparing the boat for heavy weather. We double-reefed the mainsail (reduced the sail area) that night and got everyone on a seasickness medication schedule. It was blowing crazy as hell and we had to alter course to avoid a freighter.

At 2 a.m. the wind was at its hardest and then, on a dime, it shifted 180 degrees and dropped to 15 knots. The next morning the sun dawned bright and clear. I put the mainsail back all the way up and put up the regular jib. I got some sleep after being at the wheel for 36 hours, and we had a pleasant cruise for the next five days to Tortola. Caught another fish too. Turned into a really nice sail.

The kids and Pam bounced back from the seasickness and started reading. We played Monopoly, Clue, and Go. Aspen was fine, the cats were prowling all over the place. The night sky was unbelievable.

We found out later that most of the Salty Dawg fleet had met with disaster on the rally. Some boats had to rescued and there were some injuries to other crew members that had to be air lifted to a hospital. But we had been well prepared and had managed just fine, except for a bit of cookie-tossing. We had brought enough fuel, plenty of water. This gave us renewed confidence about our ability to survive an around-the-world journey.

Persevere spent the winter down there in Tortola at Admiral Marine in Soper's Hole. We used it as home base over the Christmas holiday for three weeks.

Aspen made a reputation for himself in Tortola as the only Alaskan Malamute in the British Virgin Islands. One morning I was awoken by two children from another boat.

"Mister! Mister! Your dog killed a goat!"

Sure enough, I found Aspen lying in the driveway of the marina, proud as a lion, with a medium-sized dead goat next to him. He had dragged the poor thing 500 yards down a hill to show me his trophy. Luckily, the goat owner came by shortly. We negotiated a $300 payment for him, along with profuse apologies, and wrapped up the goat and put him in the back of the guy's pickup. Aspen's reputation quickly spread. Everywhere we went, people took pictures of him and heard the tale of the goat-killing dog.

That March I did the St. Maarten Heineken Regatta with my racing crew. It was a lot of fun and a great island to visit. Then, Memorial Day week, Breana and I and a few friends sailed Persevere back to Stamford, Connecticut. We ran into some bad weather on the 1500 mile delivery. So we diverted to Bermuda and stayed there for a few days while the weather passed.

Once we were back home, the kids started Calvert School, home schooling aboard Persevere. They will not be going to a brick and mortar school again until we figure out which continent we end up living on a few years from now.

We got a lot of experience and knowledge aboard Persevere those first few summers. We wanted to really get used to sailing and living on a boat before we departed on our big adventure. Living on a boat also helped us grow accustomed to our new life of uncertainty and "lowered" standards. Like a lot of people in the world, we have been adapting to a new financial world. My family has been living on a fraction of what we used to spend prior to the collapse. We have become more environmentally conscious and thrifty and are living a more fulfilled life. We even removed television from the household in 2010. We still have the internet and watch movies, documentaries and sports, but we've subtracted the influence of commercialism from our day to day lives. It has all been part of a four-year plan designed to coincide with the sale of our condo.

Of course, everything hinged on our ability to get out from under foreclosure and regain clear ownership of our condo. This was the last major obstacle we faced...

CHAPTER TWENTY

FREEDOM

The thing about poetic justice is that it's so damn... poetic.

Little did we know our fate would come to hinge on a strange thing called MERS. MERS (Mortgage Electronic Registration System) is a computerized system that paved the way for the whole subprime mortgage scandal. Without MERS the infamous housing bubble that ended up bursting in my face (and the faces of millions of others) would not have taken place. That's because, without MERS, there would have been no way to package mortgages into gigantic bundles and sell them all over the world at the speed of a mouse click. There would have been no way to slip millions of bad mortgages past the eyes of people paid to examine such things. The old-fashioned, paper based way of recording deeds and titles for homes was just too slow and cumbersome.

It was also, alas, too accurate, legal, and accountable. MERS did away with all that antiquated slowness and accuracy.

MERS also, in a strangely ironic way, saved my lilly white Irish ass.

You see, in the early '90s most states were badly backlogged in the processing of their titles. Banks didn't like that. It put a serious crimp on the number of mortgages they could sell. With MERS all that changed. MERS is a private company that was incorporated for the sole purpose of streamlining the recording of mortgages. By automating the processing of titles, more mortgages could be sold and bundled and resold at a much faster speed.

When MERS burst onto the scene, it began appointing "vice presidents" nationwide for a mere $25. Each VP could log into his/her own site and quickly download as many mortgage titles as he wanted, registering them instantaneously. MERS would automatically assign a number to the title so it could be bundled any way a Wall Street brokerage firm wanted. The brokerage could dissect the mortgage and take parts of it (interest and/or principle) and bundle it up with others however they wished, to get the best rating and sale price. That bundle would then get approved, as a unit, by Moody's or one of the other credit reporting agencies. The brokerage used the volume of its business with the credit agency to "encourage" the credit agency to give it great credit reports. The credit agency graded these huge bundles of mortgages without scrutinizing them very closely because it wanted the commissions and the continued business.

Everybody was making money on the system, from the bankers to the brokerage firms to the credit reporting agencies. The mortgages themselves—remember those?—were basically churned on to the next level of customer until the last owner in the secondary market got caught with a bundle of foreclosures that were worthless. All thanks to the dazzling computerized speed of MERS.

The problem with MERS is that it works on a federal level, but each state has its own recording procedures that must be followed to record a mortgage legally. If the mortgage is not recorded completely legally, then when push comes to shove it is not valid.

The MERS Corporation in Reston, Virginia has about 50 employees to verify that the recorded titles to roughly 60 million loans are correct. Think about that for a minute. Even if the employees do nothing but verify titles all day long, ten hours a day, each employee still needs to verify 1.2 million titles. How much scrutiny can one title get? Picture thousands of "VPs" across the country logging into the system and entering mortgage titles online 24/7. No way they're making any errors, right? Now add to this cluster-fuck the fact that the data in MERS has not been updated since 2009. What you end up with is a system that is understaffed, overwhelmed with data, riddled with errors, and unrecognized as legal by any state in the union.

As noted in a March 5, 2011 New York Times Article entitled "MERS? It May Have Swallowed Your Loan," by Michael Powell:

For more than a decade, the American real estate market resembled an overstuffed novel, which is to say, it was an engrossing piece of fiction.

Mortgage brokers hip deep in profits handed out no-doc mortgages to people with fictional incomes. Wall Street shopped bundles of those loans to investors, no matter how unappetizing the details. And federal regulators gave sleepy nods.

That world largely collapsed under the weight of its improbabilities in 2008.

But a piece of that world survives on Library Street in Reston, Va., where an obscure business, the MERS Corporation, claims to hold title to roughly half of all the home mortgages in the nation — an astonishing 60 million loans.

Further in the article, Mr. Powell elaborates:

How can MERS claim title to those mortgages, and foreclose on homeowners, when it has not invested a dollar in a single loan?

And, more fundamentally: Given the evidence that many banks have cut corners and made colossal foreclosure mistakes, does anyone know who owns what or owes what to whom anymore?

I love this quote of Mr. Powell; it pertains directly to my story in more way than one:

Judge Schack has twice rejected a foreclosure case brought by Countrywide Home Loans, now part of Bank of America.

...At heart, Judge Schack is scratching at the notion that MERS is a legal fiction. If MERS owned nothing, how could it bounce mortgages around for more than a decade? And how could it file millions of foreclosure motions?

Well, maybe it couldn't. Maybe that's why Chase and Bank of America, and more recently Wells Fargo, got indicted for doing illegal foreclosures nationwide.

The mortgage on our condo at 121 West 15th Street, like tens of millions of others, went into MERS immediately after it closed. It was Bank of New York (Bank of America) that ultimately foreclosed on us. So we decided, essentially, to call their bluff. Knowing something about the chinks in MERS's armor, my attorney Mathew Hearle submitted a motion, on March 11, 2008, requesting proof that Bank of America (BoA) owned the mortgage. We demanded that BoA produce the title—signed and sealed, legally, indisputably, and irreversibly. If BoA could not prove title ownership, they could not foreclose on us, right?

Well, it turned out they couldn't. So there were several delays and continuances in the courts as BoA's lawyers scrambled to prove ownership.

On January 6, 2009, BoA's attorneys submitted an email to the court that their intention was "to withdraw the motion of foreclosure and submit a new motion on the matter addressing the title issues raised."

My foreclosure was promptly disposed. By law it could be resuscitated, though, once BoA's lawyers got their shit together and verified the title—and that was what we fully expected them to do. But then we didn't hear from them again until June 21, 2013. Yes, that's right, four and a half years later. Where had they gone? A spiritual retreat in the Himalayas? Nah, probably Vegas.

The freshly resurfaced BoA attorneys submitted a motion to reopen the case but they completely failed to address the issue of the title—maybe they hoped we'd all forgotten by now—or to offer any explanation for their four-and-a-half-year absence. Judge Shlomo S. Hager promptly denied the motion on October 28, 2013, listing those issues as unresolved. He disposed the case once more. Again, it could be reopened by BoA, but the clock was ticking.

That's because the key to foreclosure in New York State is that once the acceleration of the foreclosure has begun, the mortgagor has six years to foreclose on the property and evict the tenant. Acceleration means the formal start of the foreclosure process. When the loan is defaulted upon, the mortgagor at some point tells the mortgagee in writing that the loan is now due in full, thus accelerating the loan. From this date forward, if the bank doesn't complete the foreclosure within six years it can lose both the debt and the property. A statute of limitations kicks in.

We all know the legal system is slow and in New York it is particularly slow. It is not unusual for a foreclosure to take longer than six or even ten years. So the statute doesn't affect ongoing foreclosures. As long as the case is on the court docket and has not been dismissed, there is no time limit. However, if the foreclosure is dismissed, the acceleration continues to run and if the bank is not able to restart the foreclosure anew within the six years of the initial summons, the borrower can cite the statute of limitations and have the mortgage discharged. (During this six-year period, the mortgagee must not contact the mortgage company, its lawyers, banks, or mortgage service company, and initiate any negotiations. Which is why our attorney told us never to talk to anybody and we sure as hell never did.)

On March 18th, 2014, exactly six years and one week had passed from the date the summons for foreclosure was served upon us.

Our attorneys asked the court to remove the $2,720,000 Bank of New York (Bank of America) mortgage from our condo at 121 West 15th Street.

Celebration time?

Well, unfortunately, nothing goes easily in my life, so victory wasn't as simple as I hoped. Evidently the court failed to serve a 90-day notice when it dismissed the foreclosure action (twice), as required by law. Because of the court's eff-up, the bank's attorneys could now seek to revive the foreclosure action on the grounds that the court had dismissed it incorrectly.

My family and I entered a whole new period of nail-biting as we waited to see if this latest legal glitch was going to be our undoing. After all, when it comes to law and finance, nothing is over until it's over. Open-and-shut cases can do a one-eighty at the last minute, due to the smallest of technicalities.

Fortunately for us, McCabe, Weisberg & Conway PC, the attorneys for BoA, bobbled the ball. They didn't spot the loophole that had opened up for them, and they failed even to answer the complaint to discharge the mortgage. So our council petitioned the judge for a default judgment and waited 60 days for the judge to sign it and discharge the mortgage. Finally, the court completely discharged the mortgage on June 6th 2014.

Halle-freakin'-lujah.

Finally—finally—the tide had turned in our favor. This was The Big One we'd been hoping and waiting for, for over six years. We now owned our condo, free and clear! No more living under foreclosure! No future mortgage to pay! Nothing but clear skies and sunny weather ahead.

Well almost…

There were still the outstanding issues of National Bank's lien on the condo for $250,000 and the Amex debt. But here's the thing: National Bank did not know of the discharge of the first mortgage with Bank of New York (BoA). Information is king and I wasn't about to play messenger for them. They were still under the impression that they were second in line behind a $2.7 million-dollar lien. So they figured that their chances of getting paid were slim to none in a short sale and they had already agreed to accept $25,000 in 2010 for the note. So we pressed for the latter deal with them as if nothing had changed.

Not very nice of us? Granted, but keep in mind, this loan had already been written off many years ago. The banks use these losses to their advantage, to lower their on-paper profits for tax and PR purposes. I understand it was a real loss and I understand it was my legitimate debt, but, given my experience with banks, it was hard to feel guilty about sticking it to them. The banks were making outrageous profits from bank fees and huge stock killings courtesy of zero-interest loans from the government, which they used to play the stock market. We, the taxpayers, had been subsidizing them for years while they had been cheerfully screwing us. The point is, I have lost all respect for banks, insurance companies, and the legal system. It's all a farce; a hypocritical system that cares nothing whatsoever for the interests of customers and citizens. The new mantra is "Profit at any cost." That's the only business model capitalism now respects in America. Commoditize everything, capitalize it, and exploit it. In the eyes of corporate finance, there's no more right and wrong.

So the way I see it, if you get a chance to exploit a legal loophole against the banking industry, seize it. They would do the same against you in a heartbeat. The only difference is that we don't get to go the government and ask for 700 billion dollars to cover our asses when all our customers get robbed by us.

Maybe I'm rationalizing but, hey, I'm perfectly okay with that.

My point is that anything National Bank would get in a settlement from me was now gravy for them, so getting $25,000 in cash was much better than the zero they'd get in a short sale scenario. But, after months of emails back and forth, they held fast to their original amount and will receive the judgment amount of $257,000.00 at refinancing. It was worth the college try though.

My condo was now free and clear of all liens on the title.

We were officially free! The judge's order was certified and entered into the city register.

I decided to negotiate out the American Express judgment. Amex refused to negotiate it initially and—you know what?—a Platinum card doesn't have the allure it once had. So they can keep their card and 18.5% interest. But, in the end they played ball. They already had written off the debt, so it was gravy. We finally settled on $125,000 and so ended my long relationship with American Express. I got my first card in 1986.

So finally the little guy had won one against the McBanks. After getting screwed seven ways to Sunday, we finally had something to celebrate. All systems were go for my family's big sea adventure. Unbelievable.

The condo finally went on the market in fall of 2014 for $4,150,000, which worked out to roughly $1758 per square foot. Real estate in Chelsea, at the time, was going for $1800-$1900 a square foot with a shrinking supply of 2-3 bedroom condos and a pent-up demand. We had it rented out up until June 1, 2015 to a Russian executive. He paid the full rental amount up front for six months, plus $30,000 for a damage deposit. He demanded the first right to counter any offer to buy the condo and ten days to decide. Our condo is unique. You either fall in love with it or you hate it. I had spent three months making sure everything was perfect so that he would fall in love—and it worked. Turned out, he had to have it. Problem was he didn't have the final word on his expenditures and the female powers to be would not let him bid high enough for it. IIWII. So we refinanced the condo, since it was mortgage free now and cashed out a substantial amount to pay off a lot of family debt and get our finances back in order. We kept it on the market for sale and have several parties interested, including my neighbor at 123 West 15th street. He wants to combine our condo with ours to make it a double wide as we originally planned in 2006. Funny how everything comes in full circle in the end. So now, we had our funding to start our journey.

Best of all, its tax free. When we finally sell. We will sell it under Terrapin Industries LLC which still had several million dollars in losses on its books so tax-wise Terrapin will net out and close its doors forever. The final play was to open an account in the name of Terrapin Industries LLC, take the wire transfer, and close the account out. The funds disappear. Thank you, Bank of America.

Timing was important for selling the condo because the expansion being built on top of 121 West 15th Street was due to begin in late 2015, depending on when the plans were approved by the DOB. Boy, do I miss that fun. The owner of the third-floor condo at 121 West 15th Street had bought the air rights to expand two floors on top of 121 West 15th Street and to allow the cantilevered expansion of 123 West 15th Street over the top of 121. He had submitted his plans on April Fools Day—not sure that was the wisest day to mess with the DOB—and it usually takes six months or more to get approved. Once construction starts, scaffolding will be going up, once again, on the buildings at 123 and 121 West 15th Street, and that would have killed sales on the condo until the expansion was done.

Once that expansion is complete, our condo will be worth more and the common charges will come down since they're based on each owner's relative square footage, true. But we decided it was time to depart. I partially paid off my dad and split the proceeds of my condo refinance with him. Once we sell the condo, the rest will go to a college fund for the girls, and the remainder (after settling up some smaller things) will be our nest egg, to buy a new home in whatever far-flung locale we decide to settle in. I am thinking New Zealand. They believe in green living.

#

So our real estate adventures in Manhattan, which we started in 1996, are coming to an end. We are closing the book on a major chapter in our lives. We had spent the last eighteen years trying to live our dream. Succeeding in many ways, failing in others. But at least, to paraphrase Ol' Blue Eyes, we did it our way. All but the last six years had been good and some of the last six had had their moments too. We have a lot of fond memories of 15th Street. All of our children were born there. We learned a lot about people and life there. 15th Street was a big, big part of our family's history and will always remain so. But like all places, it refused to stay unchanged and "you can never go back."

It was time to move on. No regrets. Time to start a new chapter.

We were really going to do this thing. Yipes.

I have a few projects that I will continue to promote and work on during our adventure aboard Persevere. We still need a cash flow coming in so that we don't exhaust our nest egg before we reach our final destination. So I'll continue to promote Sailors Night Vision Caps everywhere we go and work on setting up wholesale and retail partnerships abroad. Last winter, I signed up Saba Rock and Pussers Resorts in the British Virgin Islands.

We will continue to do book promotion for It Is What It Is and start a sequel about our sailing adventures. I have a series of articles being published in sail magazines on our adventure. We'll be do online interviews, TV interviews, magazine article updates, and podcasts of our family adventure through our websites www.Persevere60545.com, www.TerrapinIndustries.com and www. Terrapindesign.net.

I am also continuing to edit the seven years of film for a documentary movie. I am mastering Final Cut Pro for that purpose and am bringing along the footage on several hard drives. That'll eat up a lot of my time, but time is one thing I will have plenty of on the open ocean. I have also started a log of our family's adventures aboard Persevere to possibly do a follow-up book to It Is What It Is. Maybe call it Persevere.

The whole point of everything I've done over the past several years is to get away, explore the world, and spend time with my wife Pamela and my three daughters, Breana, Meriel, and Nerina. To make the most of our time as a family while they are still young and the world is still in one piece. The biggest thing I have learned so far in my life is that time with the people you love is the most precious asset you possess. You can never regain it once it's lost. So no regrets. Not a single one.

#

I held off on writing this final piece until the literal last minute. As I write these words, I am standing on the dock beside Persevere, holding my laptop in my hands. The sun is shining brightly and there's a brisk chill in the air. A few good friends have come to bid us farewell. We've received picnic baskets, bottles of fine single-malt, and bushels of well-wishes. Persevere is packed to the gills and ready to go. We've gone over everything a hundred times and are as ready as we'll ever be.

I ball up the "to do" list I've been carrying in pocket for the past 18 years and throw it in the trash. The act feels strangely symbolic.

Pam and the girls are all smiles, but I can see a little trepidation behind the smiles. Of course. Why wouldn't there be? As for me, those famous lines from The Shawshank Redemption jump to mind: "I find I'm so excited I can barely sit still or hold a thought in my head. I think it is the excitement only a free man can feel, a free man at the start of a long journey whose conclusion is uncertain."

Am I scared? Shitless. You bet. I mean, how often do you literally cast off your lines and sail into the sunset with no idea where and when your journey will end and whether you'll ever be back home again?

Of course, we do have our route planned for the next several months and I'll have my race schedule to give me structure and focus. We won't be just drifting aimlessly. But still, this is as wild an adventure as a family can have in today's safe world of insurance policies, bicycle helmets, and retirement plans. The ocean doesn't know or care about all that stuff. The ocean hasn't changed for thousands of years. Once we cast off, we'll find ourselves.

They say we know more about the moon than we do about the oceans; I guess we're about to find out.

Even though I've known for years that we were going to do this, there was always the chance we could change our minds, right up to the last minute. But that chance is no longer available. Momentum is carrying us forward. So be it. We will never get an opportunity to do this again and if you know anything about me by now, it's that, for better or worse, I am not one to let an opportunity pass.

As Alfred Lord Tennyson wrote in the last line from Ulysses, "To strive, to seek, to find, and not to yield."

Follow us on our new adventure on www.Persevere60545.com. Or https:// www.facebook.com/pages/Persevere60545/371527152997747?ref=bookmar ks or better yet buy the sequel. Safe travels, life is an adventure join it before it's too late, and never let the bastards win.

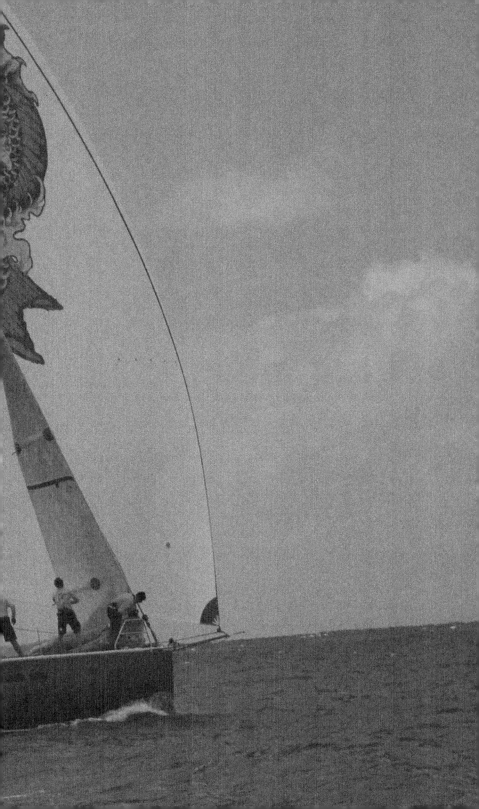

Colin Rath *It Is What It Is*:
Further Reading

Articles

Debbie, Jeffries. "The End of the Affair." Www.economist.com. November 20, 2008. http://www.economist.com/node/12637090.

Young, Jim. "Spending Boosted by Home Equity Loans: Greenspan." Www. reuters.com. April 23, 2007. http://www.reuters.com/article/2007/04/23/us-usa-greenspan-equity-idUSN2330071920070423.

Garbarine, Rachelle. "Housing Units Will Replace Armory." Www.nytimes. com. May 15, 1998. http://www.nytimes.com/1998/05/15/nyregion/residential-real-estatehousing- units-will-replace-armory.html.

McDowell, Edwin. "The Irresistible Appeal of Refinancing." Www.nytimes. com. April 6, 2003. http://www.nytimes.com/2003/04/06/realestate/the-irresistible-appeal-ofrefinancing.html.

Kiviat, Barbara. "A New Hedge For Your House." Www.time.com. September 17, 2006. http://www.time.com/time/magazine/article/0,9171,1535835,00. html.

Richards, Carl. "How A Financial Pro Lost His House." Www.nytimes.com. November 9, 2011. http://www.nytimes.com/2011/11/09/business/how-a-financial-pro-losthis- house.html.

McDowell, Edwin. "Refinancing's Extra Dividend: Cash." Www.nytimes. com. November 2, 2003. http://www.nytimes.com/2003/02/02/realestate/refinancing-s-extradividend- cash.html.

Brooker, Katrina. "What Went Wrong at One Madison Park." Www.nytimes. com. October 13, 2011. http://www.nytimes.com/2011/10/16/magazine/ what-went-wrong-at-one-madison-park.html.

Books

Randel, James A. *Confessions of a Real Estate Entrepreneur: What It Takes to Win in High-Stakes Commercial Real Estate : What It Takes to Win in High-Stakes Commercial Real Estate.* McGraw-Hill Publishing, 2008

CPSIA information can be obtained at www.ICGtesting.com
Printed in the USA
BVOW08*1952210515

401403BV00002B/2/P